BEYOND L.A. LAW

BEYOND L.A. LAW

BREAK THE
TRADITIONAL
"LAWYER" MOLD

Compiled by Janet Smith
for the
National Association for Law Placement

PUBLISHED BY

**HARCOURT BRACE LEGAL & PROFESSIONAL
PUBLICATIONS, INC.**
Editorial Offices: 176 West Adams, Suite 2100, Chicago, IL 60603
Regional Offices: Chicago, Los Angeles, New York, Washington D.C.

Distributed by:
HARCOURT BRACE AND COMPANY
6277 Sea Harbor Drive, Orlando, FL 32887
Phone: 1-800-787-8717
Fax: 1-800-433-6303

HARCOURT
BRACE
Legal & Professional
Publications, Inc.

Harcourt Brace Legal & Professional Publications offers a variety of products and services for professionals, including Gilbert Law Summaries, Legalines, Bar/Bri Bar Review and Conviser Duffy CPA Review. For a complete listing of products and services visit Harcourt Brace on the Web at www.gilbertlaw.com, or contact: Harcourt Brace Legal & Professional Publications, Inc., 176 West Adams, Suite 2100, Chicago, IL 60603. Phone: 800-787-8717. Fax: 312-782-2378.

**National
Association
for Law
Placement**

The National Association for Law Placement (NALP) is an organization of professionals involved in the career planning and recruitment of lawyers and law students. To learn more about the wide array of career planning resources available from the National Association for Law Placement, visit NALP on the Web at www.nalp.org, or contact: National Association for Law Placement, Suite 325, 1666 Connecticut Avenue, N.W., Washington, D.C. 20009-1039. Phone: 202-667-1666. Fax: 202-265-6735.

Design: Robert Aulicino/Pro-Art Graphic Design

CONTENTS

for an organization called ProKids, she has found a way to combine her skills as a litigator with her lifelong desire to do work that is in the public interest.

LAWYER BY DAY, MUSICIAN BY NIGHT _____ 37
Jorge Arciniega
(Harvard Law School, 1982)

It was the uncertainty of life as a professional musician that led Jorge Arciniega to enroll in law school. Today he balances a dual career that was the furthest thing from his mind when he was in college: he is a partner specializing in trademark and copyright law at Graham & James while continuing to perform as a professional musician—and it's not unusual for his law and music skills to be called upon in the same transaction.

MAKING A DIFFERENCE IN HER COMMUNITY _____ 41
Julia L. Johnson
(University of Florida College of Law, 1988)

Julia Johnson always knew that she wanted to engage in work that served her community but she never imagined that at age 29 she would be the youngest person and the first African-American woman ever appointed to the Florida Public Service Commission.

SUCCEEDING AGAINST THE ODDS _____ 45
Antónette Colón
(University of Connecticut School of Law, 1993)

During a childhood fraught with poverty and abuse, Antónette Colón might never have imagined her current professional success—or her current feeling of being "happy, safe, and free." But her tenacious drive, coupled with support from teachers, mentors, and friends, has enabled Antónette to succeed as a tax lawyer with the largest international public accounting firm in the world.

WORK TIME, NOT FACE TIME _____ 49
Anne Yates
(University of North Carolina at Chapel Hill, J.D., 1989;
The George Washington University Law School, Master of Laws, 1995)

Anne Yates believes that people need to "find out what is important for them." She speaks from personal experience: she found happiness as a Specialist with the Montana Department of Natural Resources and Conservation only after two successive private practice jobs in a large metropolitan area spurred her to examine her own goals more closely.

startup businesses—navigate the legal intricacies of communications, advertising, and trademark law. An especially memorable career highlight was being part of the "winning team" representing various NFL players and the NFL Players Association in litigation with the NFL.

CREATING SOLUTIONS IN A DOWNSIZED MARKET _____ 73
Jodi L. Nadler & Beth E. Fleischer
(The George Washington University Law School and Widener University School of Law)

Jodi Nadler and Beth Fleischer earned their J.D.'s in the early 1990s, during a time of extreme downsizing. But Jodi and Beth didn't succumb to the frustration that nearly immobilized other graduates. Having met each other while working as temporary attorneys, the two decided to found their own temporary attorney firm, Law Pros, which is now one of the most successful new women-owned businesses in the Northeast.

BALANCING THE MANY "SPOKES" OF LIFE _____ 77
Michael Levelle
(Willamette University College of Law, 1990)

Michael Levelle's background—which includes an unusual combination of training and experience in social work, as well as service in Vietnam—provides him with a unique perspective of the law and of life. Not content to settle for career "satisfaction," this husband and father of five has found fulfillment by balancing the many facets of his life.

AT THE HELM OF THE EPA _____ 81
Carol M. Browner
(University of Florida College of Law, 1977)

Carol Browner's work experience—including a position with the Government Operations Committee of the Florida House of Representatives; work for Citizen Action, a grassroots consumer group based in Washington, D.C.; several Congressional positions; and service as Secretary of the Florida Department of Environmental Protection—provided her with the perfect background for the top environmental position in the nation: Administrator of the U.S. Environmental Protection Agency.

STANDING BEHIND HER DECISIONS _____ 85
Kathy Boller-Koch
(University of Cincinnati College of Law, 1989)

Kathy Boller-Koch, a Magistrate with the Hamilton County Juvenile Court in

Ohio, finds satisfaction—as well as challenges—in knowing that she has the power to make decisions that can make children's lives better.

Follow Your Dream

Phil Fornaci
(The George Washington University Law School, 1991)

Phil Fornaci went to law school knowing what he wanted to do: AIDS advocacy. While working as a freelance writer, he had volunteered at Whitman-Walker Clinic in Washington, D.C., a clinic with a nationally known AIDS program. He decided he might have more impact dealing with AIDS issues if he had a law degree but never dreamed he would one day become Legal Services Director for Whitman-Walker.

Finding a Niche as a Mediator

Michael Klingler
(University of California, Hastings College of the Law, 1973)

Before Michael Klingler found his niche, career transitions were a way of life. He was a corporate accountant; a personal injury and business litigator; a staff counsel, transactional lawyer, and general counsel for a bank; a corporate chief financial officer; and a commercial real estate broker. But then he took a mediation training course and had a "wow" experience as he found a niche that built upon all of his varied skills.

Tapping Skills Developed as a Park Ranger

William S. Benish
(New York University School of Law, 1991)

As an Academic Account Manager for West Publishing, William Benish enjoys using the instructional talents he developed as an Urban Park Ranger to reach out and assist others pursuing a legal education. He coordinates WESTLAW® Training Programs for four major law schools, providing both hands-on and online instruction, and designs new programming to help law students become successful attorneys.

Doing Public Good—From Investigations to Trials

Scott D. Levine
(Northwestern University School of Law, 1988)

Scott Levine knew he had found his niche when he interned in a U.S. Attorney's Office. Today, as Deputy Chief of the General Crimes Section of the U.S. Attorney's Office, Northern District of Illinois (Chicago), he enjoys the fact that his job involves the full spectrum of trial practice—from investigations to trials to briefs to oral arguments.

ACHIEVING A BALANCE IN WYOMING
Dona Playton
(University of Wyoming College of Law, 1993)

Dona Playton landed a job where few were available—in her hometown of Laramie, Wyoming, where she is an Associate of a two-person law firm. She prides herself on her ability to balance career and family and enjoys a unique mentoring relationship with a recently retired law firm partner. Her advice to law students: "Think about who you want to advocate on behalf of."

BORN TO BE A JUDGE
Denny Chin
(Fordham University School of Law, 1978)

Denny Chin's position as a U.S. District Judge in New York City is the culmination of an unusually varied legal career, including a judicial clerkship, a four-year term as an Assistant U.S. Attorney, and private practice experience in large, medium, and small law firms. Judge Chin enjoys being challenged by the breadth of the substantive areas involved in his cases, which include not only employment law cases but also criminal law cases, intellectual property law cases, and other miscellaneous matters.

FLOURISHING IN THE SPOTLIGHT
Jerri A. Blair
(University of Florida College of Law, 1985)

Jerri Blair enjoys the diversity of her private practice, but it is her pro bono cases that have put her in the national spotlight—for example, her defense of Gregory K., the first minor to initiate a legal action to terminate his parental relationships in order to be adopted by his foster parents. Jerri has also become known for her DNA expertise, a legal area contributing to a new career twist—writing fiction and working on a movie script.

A BEACON ON BEHALF OF HER PEOPLE
Tonya Gonnella Frichner
(City University New York Law School at Queens College, 1987)

A member of the Onondaga Nation, Snipe Clan of the Haudenosaunee, Tonya Gonnella Frichner has devoted her efforts to ensuring the constitutional rights, cultural dignity, and environmental security of all Native Americans not only through her position as President of the American Indian Law Alliance, but also through teaching, writing, and numerous volunteer involvements.

CARPE DIEM... CARPE DIEM... CARPE DIEM... CARPE DIEM... ___121

Sean A. Joell Johnson
(The George Washington University Law School, 1994)

Sean Johnson has what many would consider a dream job: he is Counsel for Law and Business Affairs for MTV and is involved in all aspects of negotiating and drafting agreements related to MTV programming. His motto—*carpe diem*—flashes across his computer screen, but networking, persistence, and hard work have been the keys permitting Sean to seize the opportunities that have come his way.

A LEADER AT THE FRONTIERS OF ANALYSIS AND ACTION ___125

Jonathan Wiener
(Harvard Law School, 1987)

A public policy innovator, Jonathan Wiener drafted climate change policy for both the Bush and Clinton administrations. His zeal for the interconnections among the environment, law, society, science, economics, and human health is matched by an equal passion for community building in his own academic and civic community.

DRINK DEEP OR TASTE NOT THE PIERIAN SPRING ___129

Steven Bryan & Doug Denney
(Willamette University College of Law, 1993)

Steven Bryan and Doug Denney are law school classmates who now work for the educational software company Steven cofounded. Both attended law school without expecting to practice law. Steve launched Pierian Spring while he was still in law school; Doug joined the company later as Controller.

KEEP THEM SMILING—A CONTRACT ATTORNEY'S CREED ___135

Suzi Cohen
(Santa Clara Law School, 1977)

Suzi Cohen was a pioneer of sorts when she became a contract attorney in 1983. Customer service and client relations skills have always been among Suzi's greatest strengths, and she built upon these talents to create a very successful practice where lawyers are her clients.

After four years as a corporate tax attorney, Jay Trezevant has found his niche as the Lead Trial Attorney in the Felony Bureau of the Hillsborough County State Attorney's Office. He possesses a talent and a passion for trying cases. A wheelchair-bound attorney, Jay is pursuing a career path he had once thought impossible due to his disability.

Angela Hawekotte has masterfully combined her talents in accounting, her desire to practice law, her superb writing skills, and several years of experience at an international law firm in the successful launch of her own practice. "You make of it what you put into it," says Angela.

Mavis Thompson was both the first female and the first African-American to hold a city-wide elected office in St. Louis, a city with a minority population over 50%. As Circuit Clerk, she supervises the state courts within St. Louis, including criminal, civil, and family courts—and including 250 employees in 31 divisions.

A partner with Cohen, Todd, Kite and Stanford, Eric Kearney concentrates in commercial litigation and small business development. His own second career as President of the largest African-American publishing company in southwestern Ohio helps him understand the needs of small business owners.

Tom Condon is a columnist who writes on urban affairs for *The Hartford Courant*. He finds that his legal education has provided him with a "window into how things work" in both civil and criminal matters, and he uses this knowledge on a daily basis as he writes about the needs of the community.

HELPING NON-PROFITS ACHIEVE THEIR MISSIONS
Lawrence C. Henze
(University of Wisconsin Law School, 1988)

Larry Henze entered law school in a part-time program having already gained experience in fundraising, development, and research. He is now a successful consultant and has combined his legal knowledge with his prior expertise to help numerous institutions in the field of higher education increase their marketing potential.

A SOLO PRACTITIONER WITH A THRIVING COMPUTER CONSULTING BUSINESS
David G. Sternlicht
(Fordham University School of Law, 1991)

David Sternlicht is at a crossroads. A busy solo practitioner, he may soon need to decide which of his businesses will gain his undivided attention: his successful legal practice or his thriving computer consulting business.

AN EARLY FOCUS ON SPORTS LAW
Peter S. Roisman
(University of Connecticut School of Law, 1986)

Peter Roisman knew from the age of 10 that he wanted to be a lawyer, and from the time he entered law school he never doubted he would someday be in sports law. "Everyone told me I was crazy," Peter recalls, but today he directs the Golf Division of a company representing athletes on four continents.

SALES SKILLS CONTRIBUTE TO LEGAL SUCCESS
Diane Stehle Dix
(University of Cincinnati College of Law, 1993)

After winning national and regional awards during five years in sales-related positions, Diane Stehle Dix wondered about the wisdom of leaving a successful career for the uncertainties of law school and the legal employment market. But today the skills Diane developed in her earlier career contribute to her success as an attorney at a large law firm.

CRYSTAL CLEAR AMBITION —————————————173
Janice L. Weis
(University of California, Hastings College of the Law, 1988)

Janice Weis is Director of the Environmental and Natural Resources Law Program at the Northwestern School of Law of Lewis and Clark College. She attributes her success to the fact that she chose a field she genuinely enjoys— environmental law. "If a person chooses an area where there are a lot of jobs, but in which he or she has no interest," Janice notes, "that decision can lead to job dissatisfaction."

SUCCESS IS BEING A GOOD PROBLEM SOLVER —————————177
Kathryn A. Mobley
(University of Denver College of Law, 1975)

Few would guess now that this successful lawyer who has so many challenging options before her once dropped out of law school. But that's how discouraged Kathryn Mobley was with a first year of law school marked by rigid teaching methods and a lack of accommodation to her blindness, Kathryn not only returned to law school but went on to positions with Legal Services, with the Social Security Administration, and as a solo practitioner before becoming Assistant Attorney General for the State of Connecticut.

Contributing Authors

This book was compiled and edited by the National Association for Law Placement (NALP). Founded in 1971, NALP is a non-profit education association of ABA-accredited law schools and more than 700 of the nation's largest legal employers. NALP's member representatives number more than 1,000 and include law school career services professionals and deans, as well as legal recruitment/personnel administrators and hiring attorneys from all types of legal employers. The profiles were written by the following authors.

☐ **Diane C. Ballou** is Director of Career Services at the University of Connecticut School of Law. Prior to her present position, she was the Human Resource Manager and Attorney Recruitment Administrator for a 60-attorney law firm in Hartford, Connecticut. *(Author of profiles of Antónette Colón, Tom Condon, Michelle M. Duprey, Kathryn A. Mobley, and Peter S. Roisman.)*

☐ **Jacquelyn J. Burt, Esq.**, is Director of Career Services and an Adjunct Professor of Law at Seton Hall University School of Law. She was formerly commercial litigation associate with the New Jersey law firm of Sills Cummis Zuckerman Radin Tischman Epstein & Gross. *(Author of profiles of William S. Benish, Peter J. Carton, Jr., Tonya Gonnella Frichner, and Jodi L. Nadler and Beth E. Fleischer.)*

☐ **Kathleen A. Grant** is Director of the Career Planning Center of the University of Cincinnati College of Law. She is coauthor of *The Road Not Taken*, a book on alternative careers for law graduates published by the National Association for Law Placement (NALP). *(Author of profiles of Kathy Boller-Koch, Tracy Cook, Diane Stehle Dix, Eric Kearney, and Leslie Ostrander.)*

☐ **Hindi Greenberg, J.D.**, was a business litigator for 10 years before founding Lawyers in Transition_sm_ in San Francisco in 1985. She is nationally known for her expertise on career options and resources to help law students and attorneys identify and move forward into new career choices both in and outside law and has consulted with individuals and presented programs for bar associations and law schools across the country. She has been interviewed by *Time*, *Business Week, Inc., Forbes, U.S. News & World Report, Money, USA Today*, the *New York Times* and *Los Angeles Times,* and ABC, NBC, CNN, and PBS TV, and has had numerous of her own articles published in both legal and lay publications nationwide. Ms. Greenberg also writes a column for the State Bar of California's official publication, *The California Bar Journal*, and has recently signed a contract with a major publishing house to write a career guide for lawyers, due out in 1998. *(Author of profiles of Suzi Cohen, Michael Klingler, Elaine Lee, and Tamara Traeder.)*

❏**Laura Rowe Lane** is Associate Director of the Career Development Office of The George Washington University Law School where she has been since 1993. *(Author of profiles of Phil Fornaci, Sean A. Joell Johnson, Judith Sapir, and Anne Yates.)*

❏**Athena F. Lucero** is the Recruitment Coordinator for Whitman Breed Abbott & Morgan in Los Angeles. *(Author of profiles of Jorge Arciniega, Angela Hawekotte, Melanie McCall, and Janice L. Weis.)*

❏**Christina Meincke** is Associate Director of the Career Planning and Placement Center of Fordham University School of Law. *(Author of profiles of Denny Chin, Cathy E. Shore-Sirotin, David G. Sternlicht, and Jacqueline A. Weiss.)*

❏**Elaine Milnor** has served as Director of Admissions and Career Services at the University of Missouri-Columbia School of Law; as Assistant Director of the Boston College Career Center; and as Admissions Counselor at Regis College. *(Author of profiles of Steven Bryan, Doug Denney, Michael Levelle, Dona Playton, Tony Sullins, and Mavis Thompson.)*

❏**Cynthia L. Rold, Esq.**, is Assistant Dean for Admissions and Financial Aid at Duke University School of Law and Director of Career Counseling and Placement at Northwestern University School of Law. A past president of the National Association for Law

Placement, she has also served as the Assistant Dean for Student Affairs for the University of Illinois College of Law. *(Author of profiles of Jolynn Childers Dellinger, Gabrielle Hager, Lawrence C. Henze, Scott D. Levine, and Jonathan Wiener.)*

☐ **Ann L. Skalaski** is Assistant Dean for Career Services of the University of Florida College of Law. *(Author of profiles of Jerri A. Blair, Carol Browner, Julia L. Johnson, Charles D. Tobin, and Jay G. Trezevant.)*

The profiles submitted by these contributing authors were compiled and edited by Janet E. Smith, Director of Communications Media and Publications of the National Association for Law Placement.

INTRODUCTION . . .

Why All of These Profiles?

This book introduces 47 law school graduates who have achieved success and satisfaction through such a diverse array of career paths that they truly seem to represent an entire checkerboard of career options. In these pages you will meet entrepreneurs and dual careerists; public service and private practitioners; urban large-firm attorneys and small-town, small-firm lawyers. You will meet people who have known all their lives that they wanted to be lawyers and people who admit to "stumbling into" their decision to attend law school—people who knew their personal and professional goals when they graduated from law school and people whose goals evolved through work experiences.

You may be contemplating a career in law. Or you may be an attorney considering a transition in the career you are already pursuing. Or, perhaps you are simply interested in understanding how people develop and achieve fulfilling personal and professional goals. These profiles are neither a "how-to" manual nor a compilation of *curricula vitae*. They are instead subjective success stories from which you will learn both how this wide-ranging group of law graduates achieved success and, more important, how they define success.

Despite diverse personalities, a number of common threads emerge. Mentors, for example, played key roles for many of these law graduates— whether in the form of teachers, family members, or colleagues. Passion is another common denominator. These are people who have discovered what they want from life. Several describe a process not only of self-discovery but also of learning to give themselves permission to follow their own passions. Few landed in a dream job right out of law school. For most, success required the ability to hang onto dreams and stay true to passions through the evolving stages of their careers.

Ultimately, these profiles are a glimpse into the lives of 47 extraordinary people. Enjoy their stories as you reflect on your own dreams and goals.

Don't Fit the Mold? Create Your Own

Jacqueline A. Weiss...

If you had told Jackie Weiss as a teenager growing up in a working class neighborhood of Queens, New York, that she would later become a real estate partner at a national law firm, she says she "would have laughed." Alternately self-described as "reasonably intelligent" and as a "chatty, irreverent kid," even as a young associate at a now defunct New York City law firm Jackie had her partnership doubts. Jackie remembers, "I had this vision of what a big law firm partner was—very staid, proper, corporate—and I was none of those things. I just didn't fit that mold, I didn't want to ever make myself fit that mold and, frankly, it didn't occur to me until I was a law firm partner that I could make the mold (and so I did)."

When asked what the essential qualities of a law firm partner are, Jackie mentions intelligence, competence, commitment to the practice of law and the firm, having the respect of clients, practicing in a growth area of the firm, being a "reasonably good human being," and, beyond that, having a bit of luck on your side.

In an age when careers are sometimes microplanned, Jackie credits a large part of her success to being open to opportunity as it arose. If Jackie never specifically planned to become a big law firm partner, neither was entering real estate practice a given. A chain of events fortuitously led her in both directions. When Jackie enrolled in Fordham University School of Law, she expected to become a labor-side labor lawyer, reflecting her parents' union roots—until a high grade in her first year property class opened the door to law review and a summer associate position at a mid-sized New York City law firm. Her facility in property law also, it seems, gave her the confidence or willingness to enter the real estate department when the same firm made her an associate offer.

Jackie has found real estate practice "fascinating" and lists intellectual curiosity as a primary prerequisite because much of real estate practice goes beyond knowing simple real estate law. "Very little of it is about dirt," Jackie says, "mostly it's about finance, corporate structure, bankruptcy planning, tax issues, and perhaps municipal finance issues. You don't get stale when you need to learn a lot of things and tie them together."

Jackie made the move to O'Melveny & Myers-NY in 1988, when it was a small "branch office" that was primed to grow. "Those were the gogo days of the late eighties when every deal was a real estate deal," notes Jackie. While things have quieted down a bit since those times, she still describes the average work day for a big firm real estate lawyer as action-packed. Jackie spends a large part of her day on conference calls and in meetings, as she says, "negotiating documents and reacting, getting people to react to me, and building consensus in a way that's favorable to my client." In general, reading and writing documents make up a smaller portion of the day. Having good people skills is essential for a real estate attorney. "It can be a little like being a shrink," Jackie sometimes finds. Being a "careful, thoughtful" person with solid business judgment is indispensable as well.

O'Melveny & Myers-NY has now grown into a large office, and Jackie finds herself working on "very sexy stuff, high profile" matters that are also high stakes and high pressure. To provide a frame of reference, she notes that a "small" real estate deal now involves $10-15 million. Thus, while the pressure generated is not life or death, it can be "life shaping," as Jackie remarks, for the parties involved.

Balancing this pressure with her new family obligations is not easy, although Jackie believes her firm is more supportive than most regarding family issues. "But no matter how great one's support system is, if you want to have a family, there are trades you need to make," Jackie comments. For her this means squeezing a full day's work in by 7:30 p.m., which she has set as the time she must leave the office barring meetings or emergencies. Jackie's work day is now strategically planned and may well continue at home into the early hours after son Charlie has been attended to. Letting go of some images of perfection in both her private and professional life allows Jackie to cope. "I'm not June Cleaver and that's okay; I'm also not the most high-powered, hard-charging lawyer in this law firm. There was a time when that wouldn't have been okay with me, but it's okay with me now."

Certainly times have changed since Jackie was asked to retrieve coffee for male colleagues as a young associate at her first firm. The issues women face at law firms today, Jackie feels, are more subtle and may reflect innate prejudices, acknowledged or not. For example, people may still not be socialized to view women in leadership roles in the same way they view male leaders. Jackie has found that at all levels—and amongst attorneys, clients, and support staff—men are sometimes viewed as having more authority. Women who come on strong, perhaps in order to be taken seriously, risk being labeled "super-tough" or worse. Women may also be at a disadvantage in a firm where being a rainmaker is key. In general, Jackie says, "Women don't do business like men." On the positive side, as women now make up a larger portion of the client base, Jackie has noticed their tendency to bond more readily with women attorneys.

Jackie has attracted her client base through her proven track record (she has a reputation for being a tough negotiator), her ability to listen to potential clients carefully, and her willingness to brainstorm regarding ways the firm may be of help. "It's a symbiosis you develop with a client. Ideally it should be a partnership. Developing client trust is very important for a transactional lawyer, as more of it is trust than anything else," Jackie comments.

In retrospect, Jackie is pleased with the way her career has developed. She believes she has made the right decisions along the way and considers herself more fortunate than most. If she could change anything about the way the legal profession is evolving, however, she would slow it down just a bit. It's become too caught up in "how much, how fast," Jackie concludes. "I'd slow it down and make it more about thoughtful, careful, polite lawyering."

A NATURAL AT NATURAL RESOURCES LAW

Tony Sullins...

<table>
<tr><td>

CURRENT JOB:

Attorney and Legal Advisor, United States Department of the Interior (Boise, Idaho)

CAREER HIGHLIGHTS:

Tony Sullins describes himself as "having a fairly low-key, friendly demeanor" and believes that people like himself can be just as successful, if not more so, than the stereotypically aggressive lawyers who give the profession a bad name. Tony traces his interest in natural resources law to his childhood in the Ozarks of rural Missouri. Prior to law school, he worked as a Park Ranger and also gained experience through summer employment with the Missouri Department of Conservation. Today Tony considers law one of the best decisions he's "stumbled into," and he uses his interpersonal skills, along with a collaborative, problem-solving attitude, to make a positive difference through his job with the Department of the Interior.

</td></tr>
</table>

If anyone was ever born into the career they now enjoy, Tony Sullins would be that person. When asked how his current employer, the U. S. Department of the Interior (DOI) chose him from several hundred applicants, Tony replied, "If you took a five-year-old child and gave him all the experiences and training during his life that would make him a perfect match for a job at DOI, one version of that person would look about like me."

Indeed, the evolution of Tony's career began in his youth. "I spent my childhood running wild in the Ozarks of rural Missouri," he says. His rural background, combined with his family's experience in farming, sparked his interest in wildlife and in what Midwesterners reverently refer to as "the land." By junior high school, Tony already envisioned a career in natural resources.

Tony attended college in the rural Missouri area where he grew up. He majored in biology and worked summers at the Missouri Department of Conservation. Prior to law school, Tony spent eight months working as a Park Ranger at the Grand Portage National Monument in Minnesota. "My greatest accomplishment there," states Tony, "was to marry the Park Superintendent's daughter!"

Tony had never considered a law career, but, during his senior year of college, a friend bound for law school showed him a copy of *Barron's Guide to Law Schools*. Tony was surprised to see law school courses like "Water Law" and "Natural Resources Law." He recognized immediately that law school could offer an opportunity to combine several of his interests and decided to attend the University of Wyoming because of its strong program in natural resources law.

"Law is one of the best decisions I've stumbled into," says Tony. "Though I would have been happy as a Park Ranger or a biologist, I enjoy the intellectual challenge and the opportunity to use more of my potential in law. Every day I am challenged."

In law school, Tony was President of the Natural Resources Law Forum. He excelled academically, was a member of the law review, and published an article in his field of interest. While in school, he completed the extensive application process for a position with the DOI Honors Program and was selected. After earning his J.D. in 1992, Tony started working for the Department of the Interior, his current employer, in Washington, D.C. A year later, Tony was delighted to transfer to Boise, Idaho.

As an attorney and legal advisor for DOI, his day-to-day activities are varied. Overall, he provides legal advice for the Secretary of the Interior and for Interior's agencies, including the Bureau of Reclamation, the National Park Service, the Bureau of Land Management, and the Fish and Wildlife Service. He advises on issues such as water rights and the Endangered Species Act. For example, salmon have become endangered species in many parts of the Pacific Northwest. Tony has worked to purchase water rights from farmers to transfer the water to instream use to protect and preserve the endangered salmon. One of Tony's proudest accomplishments was being invited by the Governor of Idaho to attend the signing into law of a salmon-related water rights bill Tony had negotiated.

Tony notes that there is a slight distinction between environmental law and natural resources law to those in the field. Natural resources law concerns itself with the use and/or protection of wildlife, land, and water. Environmental law typically focuses on pollution control issues.

In addition to being happy with his career choice, Tony feels that he has been successful. "Lawyering is communication," he notes. "My strength is my ability to connect with people on a personal level. . . . You have to learn what drives a person and respect that—it's part of bringing out the best in the people around you. If you make people feel like they have a contribution to make, they are inclined to help you solve a problem."

Tony relates a story to illustrate the communication and people skills that are so necessary in lawyering—and that make law so rewarding. He visited a small Idaho town to call on the board of directors of the local irrigation district. He met them in a musty old hall down by the railroad tracks. He described the desirability of transferring water rights from the irrigation district to instream use for the protection of endangered salmon. "This is a hard 'sell' in rural Idaho, where entire communities are often sustained by irrigation water," says Tony. He then waited outside in the blazing sun for half an hour as the men haggled over the issue. They called him back inside to tell him that they would work with DOI to transfer the water rights. That is the kind of satisfaction that makes it all worthwhile for Tony.

In contrast, Tony tells another anecdote about an interview he had with a large law firm in Montana. During one long day he met with 15 or 20 people at the firm. Convinced that the day had gone well, Tony assured his wife that an offer would be forthcoming. Instead, the firm declined to offer him a position, although in her rejection letter the Managing Partner indicated that she would be willing to give Tony some feedback if he called. Tony took her up on her offer for feedback. She told him that every attorney he had met with that day liked him very much—in fact, they thought he was so "nice" that he might not be tough enough to be a good litigator, so they did not offer him the job.

In response to that mode of thought, Tony reemphasizes his convictions. "You don't need to be continuosly arrogant, aggressive, hardcore, and nasty to be a good lawyer," he says. "The best lawyers I have seen put aside the self-promotion and bring out the best in those around them, including the opposition. You'll be just as effective, if not more so, by working with people rather than against them." Tony believes that the reputation of the legal field has suffered because of the emphasis on "toughness" and because the relationship between parties in legal disputes is so often defined as adversarial rather than problem-solving in nature.

In addition to his professional accomplishments, Tony defines himself as a successful person because he has "balance" in his life. He is a husband, the father of two, and an active community member. Though he admits to being "ambitious with regards to career," Tony adamantly states, "I refuse to judge my own worth as a human being based upon my professional accomplishments alone."

As for disappointments, Tony has experienced only a few, which have come when he has not gotten all he wanted for a client. There have also been a few challenges. "When I went to law school," he says, "I was a rural, unsophisticated country boy from an impoverished background. I didn't know much about the world of attorneys. I didn't have any professional role models." However, Tony's rural background, his exposure to farming, and his practical problem-solving attitude all contributed to his success. To those who wonder whether a nice guy can be a successful attorney, Tony Sullins answers a resounding "Yes!"

Dreams Can Come True

Charles D. Tobin . . .

CURRENT JOB:

Assistant General Counsel,
GANNETT Co., Inc.
(Arlington, Virginia)

CAREER HIGHLIGHTS:

As a solid student at a solid (but not national) law school, Chuck Tobin demonstrated how following your passion can make your dreams come true. Chuck, who worked as a newspaper reporter before attending law school, has never lost sight of his love for journalism. He knew he was unlikely to land a job with a large national media corporation right out of law school, but his passion for journalism provided direction for his initial legal job search—and for a career path that has successfully achieved his goal.

Dreams really can come true. Just ask Chuck Tobin. As Assistant General Counsel for the Gannett Co., Inc., which owns *USA TODAY* as well as 92 daily newspapers, 15 television stations, and 11 radio stations, this former reporter has found his dream job. At one time, he considered this "dream job" unreachable for a University of Florida graduate with a solid academic record but without the touchstone law review-type credentials.

What enabled Chuck to ultimately land his dream job? Along with the traditional ingredients for success—hard work, focus, and ambition—Chuck also possesses a genuine passion for journalism. As a former high school newspaper editor with a keen interest in politics, government, and debate, it seemed only natural for him to gravitate toward journalism—and away from the medical profession, which was a tradition in his family. The College of Journalism and Communication's strong reputation and its brand new building on the University of Florida campus further convinced Chuck that he was heading in the right direction.

During college he increased his journalistic knowledge and skills by working as a stringer for *The Gainesville Sun* and *The Independent Florida Alligato*r. After graduation, he spent two years as a reporter and bureau chief for the *Fort Myers News-Press*. Although he loved his job, he resigned to return to the University of Florida to pursue a law degree in hopes that it would lead to greater opportunities for advancement.

Chuck readily admits, "I did not enjoy my first year of law school and didn't perform as well as I should have because I was not prepared for the commitment." As he mastered the routine discipline required in law school, he began to experience more success. At the same time, he developed a strong interest in trial practice but never lost his zeal for journalism. The summer after his first year, he began teaching basic reporting classes at the College of Journalism. There he was able to continue the mentor relationship he had established with Bill Chamberlin, his media law professor.

The following summer, Chuck obtained a summer clerkship at Gannett with a little help from his former employer, the Gannett-owned *Fort Myers News-Press*. He thoroughly enjoyed the experience but was quick to observe that their in-house attorneys had significant practice experience and impressive credentials from top-tier law schools. The prospect of working for Gannett after graduation seemed unlikely. Aware that he would need to get serious about his job search when he returned to law school in the fall, Chuck developed a strategy. He took advantage of the contacts he made over the summer and sent résumés to each of the Washington, D.C., firms with which he had come in contact while working at Gannett. That was unsuccessful. Next, he wrote to every Florida law firm with a significant media law practice. Still, no luck. Finally, with graduation looming around the corner, he began applying to general litigation firms throughout the state. It was his long-time mentor, Bill Chamberlin, who encouraged Chuck to contact a lawyer he knew at a Jacksonville general litigation firm with a small media law practice. Although Chuck was not particularly interested in Jacksonville, he mailed a résumé. He still remembers mailing that fateful letter on the Thursday of exam week and his utter surprise when he received a telephone call early Saturday morning—just two days later—from George Gabel, who was anxious to set up an interview.

The firm of Gabel, McDonald, Anderson & Dees consisted of four partners practicing in general civil litigation. They also did some local work for Gannett subsidiaries and had checked with the two Gannett references listed on Chuck's résumé. The interview confirmed that it was a great fit. Chuck was interested in trial work, he wanted the opportunity to do some media law, and his background would strengthen the firm's existing relationship with Gannett. Chuck's career focus shifted as he set his sights on gaining as much media and litigation experience as possible and becoming a vital member, and ultimately a partner, at the firm. That goal was realized after just one year with the firm, during which time he had significant client contact and the chance to try some cases.

As a partner in the firm, Chuck continued to gain trial and appellate experience in insurance defense, maritime, commercial, and media law cases. He represented Gannett as local counsel for WTLV and, on occasion, *USA TODAY*. Chuck represented several of the firm's other local media clients including the *Jacksonville Times-Union* and the *Jacksonville Business Journal*. Through his active involvement with the Media and Communications Law Committee of the Florida Bar, Chuck kept abreast of cutting-edge media law issues and was asked to teach an undergraduate course in media law at the University of North Florida. In February 1992, he had the opportunity to invite Gannett's Senior Legal Counsel to speak on a panel he was moderating on journalists' privilege at the Florida Bar's Annual Media Law Conference. Chuck obviously made a positive impression on his future boss who, in January 1993, called to make an unexpected inquiry. Gannett was creating a new in-house position and was looking for a lawyer who could litigate libel cases and privacy suits nationally for the company. They were contacting him to see if he would consider the job. After "catching his breath," Chuck said he was very interested and would discuss the opportunity with his wife and get back to them as soon as possible. Chuck accepted the position, and within a few months he and his wife moved to Arlington, Virginia.

As Assistant General Counsel, Chuck currently handles about 25% of Gannett's libel and privacy cases and is involved in decisions regarding which cases will stay in-house and which will be handled by outside counsel. He spends much of his time preparing motions to dismiss and motions for summary judgment, and collaborating with the local counsel Gannett has established throughout the country. Although he aims to keep the workload of local counsels in his cases to a minimum, he always involves them in plotting their defense and enjoys those close working relationships. In fact, a key element in his overall job satisfaction is that he considers many of these lawyers to be close friends as well as colleagues.

What makes Chuck's career such a great success story? Many would cite his impressive trial record, and, indeed, in his initial three years with Gannett, he has not lost a single case. Others would point out that he has made a name for himself as a knowledgeable and dedicated media lawyer and has taught and lectured on media law throughout the Southeast and elsewhere. Perhaps even more inspiring in an era of widespread job dissatisfaction is Chuck's fulfillment in his work and his devotion to his clients' enterprise. Chuck sums up his career satisfaction by saying, "I enjoy working for a company that is at the forefront of both journalism and media technology. It is also immensely gratifying to work almost exclusively for journalists—a group that, as with lawyers, is often unfairly maligned. As a former reporter, I understand journalists' daily work lives and, on a broader level, appreciate the importance of their role. It is a privilege—and a humbling one—to be their voice in court."

FOLLOW YOUR BLISS

Elaine Lee . . .

CURRENT JOB:

Director of the Koshland Fund, The San Francisco Foundation; Travel Writer (San Francisco)

CAREER HIGHLIGHTS:

Calling herself "a professional do-gooder" who is also "good with finances," Elaine Lee believes she has a natural talent for foundation work. Her current position also allows Elaine to pursue another interest—being a travel writer. The career path that has led Elaine to this fulfilling point in her professional life is quite different from what she envisioned when she attended law school. Yet, through all of her varied jobs—from running her own lunch shop during college to teaching law and from being a solo practitioner to directing a non-profit organization—the key for Elaine has been to "follow her bliss."

From the time she was a young adult, Elaine Lee knew she wanted to be involved in three things: helping others help themselves, travel, and writing. These are the things, says Elaine, that are "the music of [her] soul." Today she actively pursues all three interests through her two professional roles—serving as director of a foundation fund and being a travel writer. In many ways, Elaine's career path has been quite different from what she envisioned when she attended law school. Yet she has achieved a fulfilling "harmony" in her life by never losing sight of the things that provide "music" to her soul.

When Elaine earned a degree in religion from Western Michigan in 1973 and then attended graduate school for one year, also in religion, she had an express purpose in mind. She wanted to create a program to train African-American ministers to assist their communities in setting up non-profit organizations to carry out socially relevant projects. "Black churches are the most powerful institutions in the black community," Elaine comments, "and, if they can be encouraged to do socially relevant work, it could uplift the black community as a whole." Her idea was to hold summer institutes for ministers in order to introduce them to liberation theology, while teaching practical skills that would help ministers learn how to establish non-profit organizations such as food co-ops, credit unions, and senior housing.

Elaine obtained a law degree from the University of Denver College of Law in 1977 because she thought the credential would enable her to work more effectively with these ministers—the overwhelming majority of whom were male. However, while she was aware that males dominated the clergy at that point in time, Elaine recalls that she was "unprepared for the reality of sexism and found no way for a young, small, black woman to effect change on black churches nation-wide." She decided that her plan would have to wait for 10 to 15 years.

It was time to look to other directions. Elaine took and passed the Colorado bar exam in 1977, but moved to San Francisco because she was awarded a Reginald Heber Smith Fellowship to work in public interest law in the Bay Area. She spent the next two years at a branch office of San Francisco Neighborhood Legal Assistance, with her primary focus on civil legal work. Following her fellowship, she taught administrative law at New College of Law in San Francisco for two years and worked as a rent control hearing officer for the San Francisco Rent Stabilization Board—the government office with oversight of rent control issues.

Elaine's next incarnation tapped management skills she had developed during college when she ran her own business, a lunch shop in Washington, D.C., called "Elaine's Edibles." She also made use of skills she had gained while working for a family law practitioner for a year during law school. Elaine's new assignment was as Director of the non-profit Family Law Center in Berkeley—an organization which she helped to grow. In addition, after taking and passing the California bar exam in 1989, Elaine practiced some family law.

In early 1991, after 10 years, Elaine left the Family Law Center and opened a solo practice in family law and general civil matters. But, at the same time, she also "semi-retired" and traveled around the world for two years—doing only enough legal work to pay for her travel. When Elaine finished her explorations and returned to the Bay Area, she realized that she was tired of going to court. She considered the possibility of focusing her practice on several narrow areas—family mediation, for example. She also looked into getting a job in non-profit foundation management. To learn more about this second option, she took a non-profit management course. The course made her realize how much she had enjoyed watching the Family Center grow. This, in turn, gave her the idea that seeking a job in grant-making could be a way to help a non-profit organization succeed.

Elaine's next step was to develop contacts in the grant-making field. She found that the individuals involved in grant-making and foundation work that she spoke with seemed to like their jobs, so she asked some of these contacts how to go about finding an opening. She was told about the Foundation Library and began consulting their job listings—all the while continuing to look at law practice options.

Shortly thereafter, Elaine applied for a job at the San Francisco Foundation and was hired to work in the areas of community unity and leadership development as the Director of the Koshland Fund, a family fund within the larger foundation. The Fund designates money for special projects, making a five-year, $300,000 commitment to specific neighborhoods in the Bay Area. Some of Elaine's responsibilities are to cultivate leaders in various neighborhoods, give seminars to teach leadership skills, help project organizers write grant applications, plan and present proposals to the San Francisco Foundation, and coordinate efforts on collaborative projects. Elaine is delighted that she is now doing almost exactly the work she had envisioned for herself when she finished college!

Elaine says that she has "always been good with finances and is a professional do-gooder," so she believes she has a natural talent for foundation work. Because she also wants freedom of movement, it was important to Elaine to find a position that allows flex hours and independence—both characteristics of her current job. She has created an environment in which she is able to do her best work—with assistance in balancing her life, she says, from her two "canine children."

Her parallel activity while working for the Foundation has been establishing herself as a travel writer. After her world travels, she wrote and marketed an article for publication, then cultivated a book contract for an anthology on black women and international travel that will include stories and resources.

Elaine counsels those who are considering their career paths to do as the career books advise. "Follow your bliss," she says. "You need to take risks." In her own case, Elaine notes that publishing a travel article required a year of writing, researching, and marketing. But she took the chance and devoted the time and energy required for publication, and now a book contract has become part of the fulfilling harmony of her life.

Representing Baseball in Australasia

Peter J. Carton, Jr. . . .

CURRENT JOB:

Director of South East Asia, Australia, and New Zealand Operations for Major League Baseball International

CAREER HIGHLIGHTS:

A former nationally ranked tennis player, Peter Carton has followed his dream by combining his extensive talent and interest in professional sports with a law degree and a graduate degree in sports management. Peter's career path illustrates the importance of being true to your interests and keeping your dream alive.

Almost all children experience that one moment on the court or playing field when their heart is pounding and they say to themselves, "This is where I want to be in life—surrounded by the thrill of professional sports." For Peter Carton that dream became a reality. The former nationally ranked tennis player is using his law degree as Director of South East Asia, Australia, and New Zealand Operations for Major League Baseball International. In this capacity Peter manages Major League Baseball's broadcast rights, licensing, marketing, sponsorship, special events, and game development in the Australasia region.

Early in his childhood, Peter was fortunate to receive mentoring from role models in the fields of both sports and law. Born in 1966, Peter began his involvement in sports by playing soccer in his hometown of Middletown, New Jersey, but it was as an amateur tennis player—first with Christian Brothers Academy and later at Catholic University—that Peter rose to national prominence.

However, even as Peter's excellence in tennis highlighted his potential to succeed in the sports world, his pride in his family's longstanding tradition of achievement as New Jersey practicing attorneys left him leaning toward a career in law. Could he possibly blend the two fields? While numerous role models existed within each field, the blending of sports and law did not yet seem feasible to Peter. He continued to excel in tennis throughout high school. Looking to colleges in the Northeast, he chose Catholic University, where he completed a degree in financial management while vigorously pursuing his tennis achievements. He was named the R. Harris Distinguished Graduating Scholar Athlete, and he continued to achieve NCAA rankings and receive national acclaim.

"At this point," Peter indicates, "I knew I wasn't going to make a living playing professional tennis, yet I was anxious to keep up my contacts with sports." He adds, "People were asking me, 'what are you going to do when you graduate?' My family role models pointed toward the law, yet my heart was also in sports."

In an experience that illustrates the value of networking and internships, Peter linked up with a colleague of an alumni contact at PROSERV, a major sports marketing group located in Washington, D.C. During a part-time, volunteer internship while he was attending Catholic University, Peter admits he became "hooked" on the dynamic atmosphere at PROSERV. His first project was working on a Virginia Slims tournament. It was at PROSERV that Peter realized that a career that combined sports and law was not only feasible but a very exciting option. "I looked around and realized that a lot of the major people in the organization were lawyers," says Peter, "and that the importance of good analytic and communication skills that I knew law school gives you as a foundation cannot be underestimated."

While at Catholic and serving his PROSERV internship, Peter was captain of the tennis team, ranked twelfth by the NCAA, was Champion of the NCAA's Eastern Consolation Tournament (1987), and served as head tennis instructor at Rumson Country Club and as Club Champion of the Sea Bright Lawn Tennis and Cricket Club.

In Peter's senior year at Catholic, he experienced a wonderful and excruciating dilemma. He received an acceptance to law school—and he received an offer from PROSERV to come on board full-time after graduation with a promise that his first assignment would be traveling to Georgia to live with Kenny Rogers and his family while preparing for an upcoming made-for-television sports/rock all-star athletic competition. Unfortunately, the two options were mutually exclusive logistically because of the timing, workloads, and geography involved.

"It was a difficult choice," says Peter, "law school versus the sports world. I felt pressure from all sides." Peter opted for law school admission at Seton Hall University School of Law and found his niche in the school's emerging sport law program under the direction of Professor Lawrence Bershad. He served as the inaugural Editor-in-Chief of the *Journal of Sport Law*, published a sport law-related article, and coordinated the Sport Law Symposium.

It was during this period that Peter saw his tie to the sports industry solidify through his legal career. "I was constantly meeting sport law attorneys who had similar backgrounds to my own," notes Peter. Summers during law school found Peter studying international business law at Cambridge and clerking for a New Jersey law firm.

Peter's next challenge came following law school when trying to find a permanent position at the entry level in a sport-law-related field. "It was very frustrating," says Peter. "All sport law positions are highly competitive and no structure is in place to hire right out of law school. I felt either overqualified for non-law-related positions within sport or underqualified for law-related ones. I felt I had tried so hard and achieved a great deal but couldn't lock onto that first right position."

He decided to pursue a masters in sports management through a prominent program at the University of Massachusetts, Amherst. Peter received his M.S. in sports management in May 1992. During the program he served as a graduate assistant to the eminent Glenn M. Wong, Esq., Professor and Department Chair of the Department of Sport Studies at the University of Massachusetts, Amherst, and, as a graduate assistant, Peter co-authored numerous publications. He was recruited out of this program by Paul Archey, also an alumnus of the sport management program at the University of Massachusetts, Amherst, of Major League Baseball International—recruited first as a consultant and then as Director of Major League Baseball International's Australia Operations in Sydney, Australia.

Peter, his wife Susan, an account executive with Marsh & McLennan, and their daughter Mackenzie now make their home in Sydney, Australia, where, as director of operations for the Australasia region, Peter is responsible for the establishment of an independent office and the execution of all Major League Baseball activities, including licensing, marketing, sponsorships, special events, and negotiations and sales of broadcast rights. He recently conducted the Bo Jackson Australia Tour with

Nike, and he has also established a primary school baseball teaching program. Peter describes the Australian sports fan as "just as passionate" as the American sports fan. He enjoys representing the U.S. national pastime and the league's interests abroad. He equally enjoys returning to the States to see family and colleagues, attend sporting events, and, of course, play some tennis. Peter loves his work and is right where he always wanted to be. "I am very lucky," he adds. Yet, it is not luck but Peter's own expertise and enthusiasm that has kept him where he is and will continue to drive him to his goals.

LIFE AS A DARING ADVENTURE

Michelle M. Duprey . . .

CURRENT JOB:

Solo practitioner, Employment Law and Disability Civil Rights (Farmington, Connecticut)

CAREER HIGHLIGHTS:

When Michelle Duprey was born, she had 23 broken bones. Doctors told her parents, "Take her home and don't touch her. She's going to die." A victim of Osteogenesis Imperfecta, Michelle has had more than 200 broken bones throughout her life. Today, with the aid of a wheelchair and a specially adapted vehicle, Michelle is independent and is a successful attorney with her own practice. In addition to representing clients in employment matters, Michelle provides employers with workshops that assist in eliminating discrimination in hiring and in day-to-day management practices.

When asked if she has any heroes, Michelle Duprey turns to her computer and says "Helen Keller." There, on a bright blue background, a quote from Keller goes round and round—"Life Is Either a Daring Adventure or Nothing."

Michelle, like Keller, never gives up. As a solo practitioner specializing in employment law and disability civil rights, she works constantly to help others who are disabled or discriminated against. She was appointed by Governor Weicker to serve on the Connecticut Rehabilitation Advisory Council, where she represents business and industry to the Bureau of Rehabilitation Services. She also assists Bryant College with the development of employment and prelaw classes and the active recruitment of persons with disabilities and has assisted the University of Connecticut School of Law in assessing the accessibility of its new law library. When she is not serving on a committee, Michelle is writing a quarterly column for *Breakthrough*, the National newsletter of the Osteogenesis Imperfecta Foundation, Inc. She is also a member of the Osteogenesis Imperfecta Foundation Speakers Bureau.

Much of the federal law that is the focus of Michelle's practice and her speaking engagements was not yet in place during her own early years. In elementary school Michelle was segregated from other students because the school was afraid that she would continue to break bones if she attended classes with the other children. "I just missed the mainstreaming movement," Michelle comments. Despite her learning environment, Michelle excelled throughout her school years, becoming very involved in student council activities on both the state and national levels.

In 1986, when Michelle investigated 15 undergraduate schools from New Hampshire to Washington, D.C., she could find only three that were wheelchair accessible. One of those schools was Bryant College in Rhode Island, where Michelle studied business with a double major in economics and marketing. Preparing herself for a career involving international business transactions, Michelle studied Chinese; she graduated with a Bachelor of Science in business administration in 1990.

During her early years at Bryant, Michelle's father suggested that she go to graduate school immediately after college. He created elaborate spreadsheets to support his argument. Suddenly, in Michelle's junior year, her Dad passed away. In her senior year, she remembered his spreadsheets and also recalled high school dreams of becoming a lawyer. She decided to go to law school to prepare for a career as a corporate law and finance attorney.

Michelle hated her first year of law school. Asked why she didn't quit, Michelle comments, "I never give up." Once past the first year of core curriculum, Michelle looked forward to tailoring the rest of her classes to her career of choice, international business law. That all changed when she took a course called "Business Organizations" and, instead of loving the course, despised it. She knew then that a career in international business was not for her.

Michelle finally found her niche while clerking for a law firm during the school year. She worked for a small employment discrimination boutique where she was exposed to both plaintiff and defendant work. She was assigned the task of screening and writing up the details of at least 10 to 15 incoming client telephone calls per day, and when the office manager left, she assumed responsibilities for managing the firm and training paralegals. Little did she know that the law firm management skills she was learning—some of which "didn't seem a bargain at the time"—would become very useful in the near future when she built her own practice.

Michelle recalls that her only "A" during law school was in trial practice class. An adjunct professor who was a seasoned litigator eliminated her fears of the litigation process. After graduation Michelle faced another obstacle—the bar exam. On her first attempt Michelle failed the test, though only by a few points. True to her independent spirit, she had not thought to ask for any accommodations. Unfortunately, the writing table was not the right height for her as she took the two-day exam sitting in her wheelchair. Michelle resolved not to take the exam more than twice. "The second time was going to be my last," she says. She talked to members of the bar examination committee, and they let her take the exam at one of their offices in a wheelchair-accessible room where the desk height was properly adjusted. She passed easily on the second try.

Following law school, Michelle was asked to become an associate at the firm where she had been clerking. Two years later she left the boutique, hoping to land a job with a larger firm. She didn't plan to open her own practice. However, two clients insisted she continue to work for them. She worked from home and soon got two more referrals. Before long Michelle was concluding "I guess I'm in business for myself" and arranging for better office space.

Private practice as a solo practitioner has enabled Michelle to tailor her schedule to her own work style and to client needs. She works seven days a week by choice but has the freedom to leave early on Friday if she wishes. Michelle says, "You have to call clients on weekends," and she notes that often "it is the only time they can come by."

Finding that she works best in two-hour stints, Michelle typically arrives at her office around 9:00 a.m. and begins the day by checking her e-mail and voice mail. After two hours, she takes a break, socializing with others in the office complex. The only attorney in her building, she occasionally gets work referred to her from others in the building, so she finds these "breaks" to be good for business. When she returns to her office, she talks to clients and drafts documents. Michelle takes another coffee break around 3:00 p.m., then works two more hours. On days when she is not seeing clients, Michelle takes her dog to work to keep her company. Active in community and professional organizations, Michelle typically attends about three meetings a week outside her office. Because of the flexibility she has built into her schedule, she does not think that she will ever again be able to work for someone else.

Today, Michelle likes the law and enjoys what she is doing. While she found that law school placed the emphasis on citing case law and researching, Michelle feels her legal practice is more a matter of giving her clients practical advice to make their lives better. She formulates a plan for her clients to follow, which gives them a sense of empowerment and encourages them to become proactive, busy, and productive.

Using her marketing degree to increase her client base, Michelle enjoys the business side of her practice as much as she enjoys the practice itself. In order to have a successful practice, according to Michelle, "You need to have a continuous flow of clients. You must always be marketing and understand the fixed and variable costs involved in running a business. You need to know all this to know how much you need to be charging." She wishes she had read Jay Foonberg's book, *How to Start and Build a Law Practice*, before she began her practice, but when she picked up a copy of the book after she was already well established, she discovered she had "actually done everything right." Michelle's involvement in local organizations and her speaking engagements are both sources of new clients. In addition, smaller cases are referred to her by lawyers with larger employment discrimination practices.

Plaintiff's employment discrimination cases comprise most of Michelle's practice, but she has no problem representing an employer in a wrongful suit. She gives people who come to her with their problems a little bit of hope. "It happens with every client,"she says; "their ego is so low." Everyday when a new client calls, Michelle says to herself, "This is the worst possible thing that can happen to anyone." The next day, however, she will receive a call describing something even worse. For example, one of her clients, a day care worker, had congestive heart failure and spent several days recovering in a hospital intensive care unit. When the client was transferred to a regular room and could have visitors, her employer came to the hospital and fired her. Another disabled client asked her employer to make the office bathroom more accessible and was told, "Train yourself not to have to go to the bathroom while you are at work." Michelle notes, "All that most people want is an apology or their job back—some very simple things."

Ten years from now Michelle Duprey may not be practicing law. Her hobby is cooking, and her specialty is pies. She takes them to work and people love them so much she has been encouraged to open her own pie business. One of her all-time favorite free-time activities is curling up with a copy of *Bon Appètit* in search of new recipes. She says, "That's my retirement dream job." She also hopes to become more involved in the Women and Disability Network, where she presently serves as chairperson on the board of directors.

SEE THE BEAUTY IN EVERYTHING

Judith Sapir . . .

CURRENT JOB:

Senior Commercial Counsel, Overseas Private Investment Corporation (Washington, D.C.)

CAREER HIGHLIGHTS:

Judy Sapir attended law school as a single mother of three and still managed to make law review and to graduate second in her class. She now works as an attorney in international project finance for OPIC. Prior to landing this job, she worked for a large law firm and served as in-house corporate counsel at a high-tech corporation. Judy persevered in the face of numerous obstacles and now enjoys a prosperous and fulfilling career as an attorney.

"The work is interesting and challenging, and I'm doing something good for society," Judith Sapir says with enthusiasm. She has been Senior Commercial Counsel at the Overseas Private Investment Corporation (OPIC) since December 1995. OPIC is a small U.S. government agency that finances and insures investments in developing countries. In her position, Judy supports the foreign policy of the United States government—becoming involved, for example, in such issues as workers' rights, environmental compliance, and the positive economic impact of projects OPIC chooses to finance. Judy enjoys the "value of the work" most—she helps people in developing countries and helps U.S. companies expand abroad.

But there is a great deal more that Judy finds gratifying in her job: the pleasant, intelligent people; the number of female attorneys in the legal department; the amount of responsibility; a team approach to each project; the chance to travel internationally to places like Russia, Belize, and Brazil; and a choice in work projects. Moreover, Judy likes and respects her co-workers and feels very comfortable at OPIC. All of these factors make Judy's work life interesting. She thrives on the variety and on interaction with her co-workers. She loves her job despite the fact that it is, in certain ways, more intense than her previous law firm job: She has no "down time" at OPIC, and her hours are typically comparable to those at the firm.

When Judy decided to enroll in The George Washington University Law School, she didn't really know what she would do as an attorney. She initially attended law school to solve the problem of finding a challenging professional job that compensated her in an amount equal to the time she devoted to it. She felt law school would provide a "credential for a good job." Judy didn't really know if she would like studying the law, and she admits that she "didn't really think through becoming a lawyer." However, she had always enjoyed being a student and imagined that law school, at the very least, would be intellectually stimulating.

Judy was fortunate enough to have a neighbor who worked at a large D.C. law firm and acted as her mentor. He helped her with everything from choosing a law school, to encouraging her to try out for law review (even when she didn't want to), to helping her choose which firms to drop résumés with during the recruiting season. Ironically, he was a GW grad.

Judy had entered GW as an evening student, married and with three children ages 9, 12, and 14. She excelled at GW and basked in the academic atmosphere. Judy and her husband separated at the end of her first year of law school, and she switched to the day program. She says of the switch, "I realized I needed to finish as quickly as possible and start making money."

The average student finds performing well in law school to be a challenge, yet, amazingly, Judy—though going through a divorce and parenting three children—prevailed. How did she do it? Judy admits that there was "a lot of work in law school,"and she adds, "I am a serious student— I even read everything." She says she didn't really know what to expect and had no preconceived notions about law school. She never suspected she'd do so well. As to reasons for her stellar performance, she credits at least in part the fact that she is very organized. "Going to law school and being a lawyer are not easy," she comments. But she had goals to accomplish and was very directed. Her motivation, she says, was that "she really enjoyed being in school." Still, she faced the challenge of parenting children whose needs could not be scheduled. "I was never 'off,' " she says; "I always had at least one of the girls with me." When she had just one child with her, they would often go to the library together and do homework.

Judy says she has "always tried to seek a balance in her life" and has always known that "work is not the only thing." As a lawyer, she protects her private time and schedules it as carefully as she schedules meetings. Judy also tries to separate the personal and professional. However, she tells the story of a time during her tenure at a large D.C. law firm when for 8 to 10 weeks she was assigned to a big case that required her to work very long hours. She left home before her three girls got up, and she arrived home after the girls were asleep. One night, while Judy was working in the conference room at a dinner meeting, a co-worker outside the conference room waved for her to look outside the window. There stood her three children. They had come to Judy's office to see their mom. Judy laughs as she says, "They came to visit me."

Today, Judy's children are adults. The oldest is 28 and is a physician in family practice; the middle child, 25, is a social worker with a non-profit organization and counsels children who are in trouble with the law; and the youngest is 23 and works at Hillel at Kent State University doing outreach. Judy is very proud that her children have done so well and that they are good friends. She also is proud that she has been able to obtain the kinds of jobs she wanted throughout her legal career—and of her ability to support herself in the lifestyle she has chosen.

Judy's motto for living is something she arrived at only in recent years: "Try and see the beauty in everything and enjoy it for what it is. Take the time to see what's there and reflect on the wonder of the experience of it. Life whizzes by, so look at what's really there and what is important." Judy recalls a time when she was working for a law firm and was in the lobby waiting for the elevator. A gorgeous bouquet of flowers was sitting at the reception desk. A partner walked up to wait for the elevator, and Judy said, "Aren't those beautiful flowers?" The partner replied, " I don't have time to look at the flowers." Judy stepped into the elevator and hoped there would never come a point when she wouldn't have time to look at the flowers.

In addition to working hard at a job she enjoys, Judy volunteers—something she has always done since becoming an attorney. Formerly, she gave her time to the Women's Legal Defense Fund and more recently to the Montgomery County Commission for Women. She is part of a legal callback program that gives advice—primarily to women—on legal issues.

Judy Sapir is happy not only with her challenging job but also with her family, her volunteer activities, and her lifestyle. She has found balance and an appreciation for life.

RISKS WORTH TAKING

Jolynn Childers Dellinger . . .

CURRENT JOB:

Associate, Tharrington Smith
(Raleigh, North Carolina)

CAREER HIGHLIGHTS:

In the four years since her law school graduation, Jolynn Childers Dellinger has experienced what seems like nearly a career's worth of opportunities: a federal appellate clerkship, a year-long fellowship in the Solicitor General's office during which she argued a case in the Fifth Circuit, a year at a high-powered D.C. litigation firm, and, most recently, work for a small firm in North Carolina practicing family law. While Jolynn feels the "expected" things she has done have been rewarding, the risks she has taken have turned out even better.

Jolynn Childers Dellinger views herself as a counselor and adviser as well as a lawyer. She practices family law at Tharrington Smith, a law firm of 21 attorneys in Raleigh, North Carolina. She knows that people who seek the assistance of attorneys in domestic matters—such as separation, divorce, custody disputes, or situations involving domestic violence—are often going through some of the most difficult experiences in their lives. She would like to cultivate, to the extent possible in an adversarial field, a nonadversarial approach that will make the involvement with the legal system as painless as possible for the people she works for. In the future, she would like to learn how to mediate and to help look for solutions to domestic problems, such as the creation of family courts that can minimize the stress on the individuals going through domestic problems.

Jolynn took an interesting route to reach her current position. After graduating from Columbia University with a B.A. in English, she worked as a paralegal at Cravath, Swaine & Moore in New York City for a year. She then attended Duke

University School of Law, where she participated in the joint degree program and received her law degree and a master's degree in humanities, concentrating in women's studies. "I expected that I could change things and make a difference," she says, recalling her law school years. "That's part of the reason I pursued women's studies. I thought the joint degree program in law and women's studies was a way to have the knowledge, way, and path to make a difference to specific women and their lives."

During law school, Jolynn worked with battered women and advocated on behalf of children. She also co-chaired the Frontiers of Legal Thought Conference, which dealt with race and gender issues. During the summer after her first year of law school, she got a job with the State Bureau of Investigation in North Carolina, where she researched the law on child abuse and conducted a study on sexual harassment and sexual and racial discrimination in the Bureau. During her second summer, she was a summer associate with Shea & Gardner, a Washington, D.C. law firm. Shea & Gardner offered her a position after graduation, which she deferred while she pursued two clerkships.

After law school she clerked for Judge Francis D. Murnaghan, Jr., of the United States Court of Appeals for the Fourth Circuit. She then was selected as one of four Bristow Fellows for the Office of the Solicitor General. The Solicitor General's Office represents the United States Government in all Supreme Court litigation and has to grant permission any time any of the U.S. Attorneys' offices wants to appeal a case to the United States Supreme Court. As a Bristow Fellow, Jolynn wrote recommendations to the Solicitor General regarding whether various appeals should be allowed. She also wrote oppositions to petitions for *certiorari* and assisted with research on merits briefs that were submitted to the Supreme Court. She also had the opportunity to write an appellate brief and argue a criminal appeal before the United States Court of Appeals for the Fifth Circuit. Working for the Solicitor General's Office was, according to Jolynn, "an amazing way to learn about the Department of Justice from the top down." Having been an English major at Columbia and a note editor for the *Duke Law Journal* while in law school, Jolynn was an excellent writer. She nevertheless felt that her writing skills were greatly enhanced during her time at the Solicitor General's Office. "It was a great mentoring type of job," she comments.

After completing her two clerkships, Jolynn returned to Shea &

Gardner, where she worked with brilliant people on intellectually challenging work. After she had been with her firm for only one year, however, Jolynn's husband, also a lawyer, received a job opportunity in North Carolina that he could not refuse, and they decided to move.

At that point, Jolynn began thinking about what she really wanted to do with her legal education. She contemplated many different ideas including returning to school for a Master's in Social Work, going in-house for a corporation like Glaxo, working as a prosecutor in a local District Attorney's office, obtaining some type of job in university administration, or staying with more traditional law firm practice. "I realized that I am a lawyer who is more interested in the subject matter than in the process," Jolynn explained. Thinking back on law school and her experience in Washington, Jolynn realized that some of the work she had found most rewarding had been her work with women and children and pro bono cases dealing with custody issues. Ultimately, she decided to stay in the legal field, and she narrowed her search for legal jobs to the area of family law. She carefully selected a firm with a well-established family law practice, and, after interviewing, was offered a position with Tharrington Smith to be the third attorney in the firm practicing family law full-time.

In retrospect, Jolynn acknowledges that, while in law school, she "got on a treadmill" and followed the expected path. Because she performed well at a national law school, that path was to be an editor on the law review, to be on the moot court board, to be a summer associate with a prestigious firm, and to pursue a federal appellate clerkship. While she feels lucky to have had each of those opportunities, and while she would take each of them again if offered, she suggests that it was easy to go on automatic pilot during those years and to lose sight of her original vision or of ideals that she brought with her when she came to law school.

When it came time to make an actual career decision and to decide how she wanted to practice, she admits that she didn't take the opportunity to consider the reasons she went to law school or the interests in women and children, sex, gender, and race issues that made her legal education compelling. The path that she chose led her to an outstanding D.C. law firm with a reputation for scholarship, excellent writing, and appellate advocacy. While that job provided an opportunity to learn about a national practice and work with great people, it did not draw on her interests in women and children and focused more on research and writing than on contact with clients. Thoughtful consideration of alternative career choices when presented with the need for a geographical move led Jolynn to a job that she had not considered in law school but that reflects her interests in women and children's issues. Although the career change was unexpected, she loves her job at Tharrington. "I feel like I can make a difference here," she says. "I like helping people and having a job that involves human interests."

An Advocate for Children

Tracy Cook . . .

CURRENT JOB:

Attorney Guardian Ad Litem for ProKids (Cincinnati, Ohio)

CAREER HIGHLIGHTS:

Evidence and trial practice courses during law school convinced Tracy Cook that she wanted to be a litigator. But, for as long as she can remember, Tracy has also wanted to work in the public interest. Following law school, she gained valuable knowledge of the legal system as Legal Administrator for the Hamilton County Recorder's Office in Cincinnati, but she continued to be drawn to other forms of public service. Tracy didn't wait for another paid position to open. She began volunteering for ProKids, and one year later ProKids became her new employer. Her job allows her to make a real difference in the lives of children and their families and permits her to participate in the "battle of litigation" she continues to love.

"Feeling like I'm making a difference and am involved in work that matters, dealing with lives and futures, not property and dollars" is what brings Tracy Cook satisfaction. She is an advocate for children through her position as Attorney Guardian Ad Litem for an organization called ProKids. "Never-ending demands of battling bureaucracies, challenging those around me and myself to be more effective," Tracy says, make her feel that she is truly contributing. To the observer, Tracy Cook is immediately impressive as someone who is confident and comfortable with her life. She is always smiling and always responsive, though her colleagues will tell you that she is also always late.

"I have been interested in public interest work as long as I can remember," Tracy comments. "My family constantly discussed politics and current events and issues." As an undergraduate at the University of Cincinnati, Tracy decided that political science was the major that most closely fit her interests; she minored in fine arts. During college, as Research Assistant to Dean Tom Gerety, Tracy conducted in-depth research into the permissibility of group defamation and the viability of race-remedial programs at universities in light of the Constitution's free speech guarantee and equal protection clause. She then worked for a local politician. These experiences sparked an interest in law and contributed to Tracy's decision to attend the University of Cincinnati College of Law. Two other college involvements—serving as resident advisor of a large dormitory and working with the Upward Bound Program for disadvantaged, bright high school students—though seemingly less related to becoming a lawyer were very influential in shaping Tracy's eventual career path.

When asked about her aspirations and expectations regarding law school, Tracy comments, "I wanted to learn the law but was unsure how I would use my legal education. I knew I wanted to somehow serve the public interest." Once in law school, she often felt as if she were the only one with those aspirations. "I was dismayed," she comments, "by how few of my classmates were interested in public interest law, and I questioned my own interest in this area." Moreover, after her undergraduate work experiences with Upward Bound and as a dormitory resident advisor, Tracy was dismayed to find that the opportunities that were posted on the job boards in law school seemed to reflect only positions open in law firms and corporations. "I had to give myself permission to do what I wanted, what fulfills me," Tracy comments, "and not be influenced by others' expectations." She adds: "I believe most law students feel as if they should chase dollars rather than their hearts. You've got to be your own person and not let law school mold you."

Convinced that she needed to find her own path to success, Tracy spent time in the career planning center during her final year of law school looking for career opportunities that would value her interests. She considered which classes had motivated and excited her. "I knew from evidence and trial practice courses," she says, "that I wanted to litigate." Tracy took time to meet with attorneys who were practicing in her areas of interest. She researched practice areas and built confidence in her ability to contribute her skills and experiences in a productive and proactive way.

For two years following graduation from law school, Tracy was the Legal Administrator for the Hamilton County Recorder's Office in Cincinnati. She was performing a public service but found that the subject matter of the work was not particularly engaging. "I began," says Tracy, "to selfishly think about how I could make the most impact."

Reflecting on her past experience with Upward Bound, Tracy decided she wanted to continue to work with children—to continue teaching and educating. "I realized," comments Tracy, "working with children would provide me with the greatest chance of, in some small way, changing society for the better." Having made this decision, Tracy didn't wait for a paid position to open. She explains, "I began volunteering with ProKids—an agency which provides representation for children who are the subjects of abuse, neglect, and dependency proceedings. I became an attorney at ProKids after volunteering for about a year."

During the year she volunteered at ProKids, Tracy's caseload was only a small portion of the one that she manages as a full-time staff member. Nevertheless, the volunteer caseload had seemed to require more and more of her time. As a volunteer, Tracy recognized the benefits of her experience in the Hamilton County Recorder's Office. She had gained a wide range of organizational and administrative skills, she understood the local court system, and she now knew the importance of understanding "the system." She also understood that ProKids needed to make the system work for the child's benefit.

Tracy's experience at ProKids has convinced her that it is the system that needs to be challenged and the family that needs to be educated in order for change to occur. "Cycles break with the child," Tracy explains. "If you give the parent first shot at changing their approach, then they will teach the child." At ProKids, Tracy sees children who are really damaged by abuse and neglect. She comments: "You need to find that delicate balance: be involved but not so involved that you cannot separate yourself. Your goal as the child's advocate is to provide them with the best opportunity."

Tracy believes that her position at ProKids is a direct result of having volunteered for the organization for a year before becoming part of the staff. Today Tracy continues to believe in volunteering and is involved with Volunteer Lawyers for the Poor.

"I love the battle of litigation, not just the subject matter," Tracy answers when asked what has motivated her in her career since law school. She is combining the best of her skills and energy to make a difference for children and their families. The qualities that she admires in her peers—"competence, honor, and drive"—are also the qualities that shine through when Tracy Cook talks about her work. The children and families that she meets benefit not only from her advocacy on their behalf but also from the quality of the person who is Tracy Cook.

LAWYER BY DAY, MUSICIAN BY NIGHT

Jorge Arciniega . . .

CURRENT JOBS:

Partner, Graham & James LLP (Los Angeles); Professional Musician

CAREER HIGHLIGHTS:

Jorge Arciniega is as dedicated to his work as an international corporate lawyer as he is passionate about his love for music. He works hard enduring the pressure and long hours of his thriving intellectual property practice. He plays hard, too (a musical instrument, that is). Jorge has performed with top artists including Stevie Wonder, Gladys Knight, Tito Puente, and Natalie Cole, to name just a few. Often he considers the other hat he wears as a professional trumpet player to be the secret to his success as a lawyer—helping to balance a career that was the farthest from his mind when he entered college.

Some of the best things that have happened to Jorge Arciniega were the unexpected. On the road to becoming a music performer, Jorge stumbled into a second career as a lawyer. A music major turned psychology major turned law student, he often thinks about the nearly accidental decision he made to become a lawyer, a job he has enjoyed since graduating from law school in 1982. He never had a driving passion to pursue a law career and didn't even consider it until late in his junior year at UCLA.

Even though Jorge was involved in music all his life and wanted to be a professional musician, the theoretical aspects of his music coursework didn't excite him and allowed him little time to play his instrument. By switching to a major in psychology, he had time to do his homework and coursework and still have five hours left over in the day to practice.

Soon the thought of graduate school came into the picture. Once he began penetrating the music industry in Los Angeles, Jorge began to get a real taste for the life of a musician. "The road to the top of the music industry, especially as an instrumentalist, is arduous and filled with playing bar mitzvahs, weddings, and funerals," he comments. "The recipe for success is equal parts talent, hard work, and who you know." It was the uncertainty of the profession—never knowing where his next job was going to be—that made Jorge think that there had to be a more secure way to make a living yet have enough time to play the type of music he enjoyed.

Jorge picked the brains of a few musicians he knew who had gone to law school. Math was not Jorge's strength, and when he learned that very little math was required in law school he made his decision to apply. "It was as arbitrary as that," he says.

He applied to ten nationally known schools and received acceptances from all of them except Harvard. Just before classes started at the school he was planning to attend, Jorge learned that his acceptance at Harvard had been lost in the mail for months. He received it in time to enroll, canceled his previous plans, and immediately headed east. He arrived in Boston one week before the start of the fall term with a suitcase in one hand and his trumpet case in the other.

While in law school, Jorge met other Latino students who shared concern about what role they should play as future leaders in our society. "What a minority student should do after graduation," he recalls, "was the preferred subject of debate, altercation, and fist fights." Should a minority student get a public interest job or "sell out" by working for a large private law firm? "I struggled a lot with that," says Jorge.

After working as an intern at a legal aid clinic and the National Health Law Program, Jorge decided he could best fulfill his responsibility by becoming a successful lawyer in the so-called "white establishment." When he finished law school, Jorge decided to fund an annual college scholarship to promising Latino high school seniors in the name of his parents (his father had been an undocumented field worker).

Once he made the decision to go into private practice, Jorge considered the notion of businesses and cultures coming together and the ways lawyering played a role. He sought out a firm with an international practice. His bicultural background (he was born in Tijuana, Mexico) and his fluency in Spanish made him a natural for corporate international work.

Jorge started his law career at the Los Angeles office of Graham & James, then a small office struggling to make it in a depressed legal market. After two years, he left to work at Whitman & Ransom (now Whitman Breed Abbott & Morgan). Twelve years later he has gone full circle, returning to G&J to head the trademark and copyright section of the office's intellectual property practice group. The firm now boasts one of the country's largest intellectual property practices among general practice law firms.

As a first-year associate, Jorge experienced the typical stages of pressure and insecurity. He found that three years of law school provided him with only the most meager tools required for success in a large law firm. In addition, as he saw his classmates joining society and business clubs, he realized that his nocturnal world of night clubs, recording studios, and jazz musicians was not likely to furnish him with the business contacts essential for a transition from associate to partner. Nevertheless, his music career was what provided the emotional and creative outlet Jorge needed to ease the pressures of being a young associate at a large law firm.

His gravitation toward intellectual property law as a specialty was also an arbitrary decision. In his second year of practice, he was assigned to work with a senior partner on an important trademark litigation case. He spent that year immersed in trademark law. As a result of his newly acquired knowledge, he was picked to develop that expertise in the office.

A glance around Jorge's office reveals genuine contentment with his life as attorney/musician. On the walls hang framed posters or photographs of those who inspire him, including legendary jazz great Clifford Brown and Russian composer Igor Stravinsky.

Although he does not practice entertainment law *per se*, it's not unusual for his law and music skills to be called upon in the same transaction. For example, last year his client Ernie Fields, Jr., a music contractor and promoter in Los Angeles, asked Jorge to negotiate an appearance by Ray Charles, Boy George, and several other performers in Osaka, Japan. By day, Jorge negotiated with the concert promoters and artists' agents; by night he rehearsed with Ray Charles' band. At the concert, between sound check and dress rehearsal, he handled last-minute negotiations and felt at ease knowing his firm's Tokyo office was close by in case expertise in Japanese law was needed.

Ernie remarks that "Jorge has a vast knowledge of the law . . . but what sets him apart for my needs is that he knows music and us musicians. When I hired him to negotiate the contract for Phil Collins' band, Jorge knew what issues were important for the band members and did not waste time on unessential or theoretical legal points." Jorge is equally capable as a musician. "When he plays," says Ernie, "he's as cool as can be, yet the energy and the concentration are there."

Combining both professions successfully makes for very long days. Jorge starts work early, usually by 5:30 a.m., which allows him to communicate with clients on the East Coast and in Europe. Two or three nights a week he'll have night club performances lasting until 2:00 a.m. Playing music energizes him. His two very different disciplines create an important balance . . . the yin and yang . . . in his life. "Being immersed in one makes me appreciate the other much more," he asserts. Without his music, he is convinced that he would not be the successful lawyer he is today.

MAKING A DIFFERENCE IN HER COMMUNITY

Julia L. Johnson . . .

CURRENT JOB:

Commissioner, Florida Public
Service Commission
(Tallahassee, Florida)

CAREER HIGHLIGHTS:

At age 29, Julia Johnson was
both the youngest person and
the first African-American
woman ever appointed to
the Florida Public Service
Commission. The skills Julia
learned during law school and
the training she acquired while
working for state government
have enabled her to fulfill her
lifelong goal of making a real
impact on her community.

Commissioner Julia Johnson always knew she wanted to serve the community and work for the people. She just never imagined it would be in her current role at the Florida Public Service Commission.

As an undergraduate in business administration, Julia knew she wanted to someday make an impact. Ultimately, she decided that a law degree was the best vehicle. "I saw a law degree as a means of broadening my skills while also providing flexibility and legitimacy. When I looked around at who the spokespeople were—especially in the black community—it seemed that it was typically the lawyers or the preachers," she said.

While attending the University of Florida College of Law, Julia began to "feel the pressure" to practice with one of the large Florida law firms that offered prestige and top salaries. She decided to focus on corporate and land use law, preparing herself to accept a position with a respected Orlando law firm. Once at a firm, she began to feel frustrated by how little she could actually contribute. "My real world experience was just so limited," she said. "I just didn't know enough to make any significant contributions." The law firm experience did, however, provide her with the opportunity to work with some young attorneys at various state agencies, and she quickly saw that they were getting real world experience much faster and making an impact much earlier in their careers. Although it was not an easy decision to give up her comfortable salary, Julia decided to take the risk in an effort to maximize her potential—and she has never looked back!

Julia left her firm to accept a position as Assistant General Counsel with the Florida Department of Community Affairs, where she was responsible for analyzing proposed Developments of Regional Impact (DRIs) and preparing relevant legal documents, advising the Governor's Office on growth management issues, and mediating and negotiating with local officials and citizens on land use issues. She quickly gained the experience she wanted—often by trial and error—and was energized by the level of responsibility she was given.

When William Sadowski, a former state legislator, was named Secretary for the Department of Community Affairs, Julia found she had a great mentor in her new boss. Sadowski was returning to the public sector following a stint in private practice. Among other things, he shared with her that "young lawyers always want to save the world; the best way to do that is by being proactive in the process where laws are written—the legislature—rather than litigating on a case by case basis." His words inspired Julia to move on to the position of Legislative Affairs Director within the Department. As chief lobbyist for the Department, she was now drafting legislative proposals, analyzing bills before the Legislature, and representing the Department at legislative hearings. Her areas of expertise grew beyond land use and growth management to include economic development, energy efficiency, housing emergency management, and wastewater issues. Clearly, Julia was making an impact and serving the community and people as she had set out to do. But just one year later, she was offered a new and even greater challenge when she was appointed by the Governor to a four-year term on Florida's Public Service Commission.

At age 29, Julia was both the youngest person and the first African-American woman ever appointed to the PSC. As one of five commissioners, she helps set the rates and regulations for Florida's four-billion-dollar, investor-owner utility industry, which includes electric companies, gas utilities, water and wastewater systems, and telecommunications providers. Julia appreciates the uniqueness of the PSC's quasi-judicial, quasi-legislative role and enjoys being in a position where she and her fellow commissioners hear arguments from lawyers and from the public before making administrative rulings on the issues.

Needless to say, Julia no longer feels frustrated by a career that was moving too slowly and not allowing her to make the contributions to which she aspired. Her law degree and her three years at the Department of Community Affairs equipped her with the skills and expertise to serve and to make an impact. Additionally, she feels her age, gender, and background all enable her to bring a fresh perspective to the job. "People my age view things from a different perspective," Julia commented. "Just because something has always been done a certain way doesn't mean it has to stay that way. I may ask naive questions, but I hope my naiveté opens a new dialogue."

Julia is frequently invited to speak to college students and law students. She encourages them to get involved in state government, where they can not only make a difference but also gain valuable experience that will enable them to command a higher salary down the road. "Given my experience, I probably could earn more right now if I were back in private practice," she remarked, "but I'd be willing to do this job for free, so I believe I'm still coming out ahead!"

Julia has been reappointed by Governor Lawton Chiles for a second term. She will serve as Chairman of the Commission during 1997 and 1998. "Although I never imagined I'd end up here, I'm doing exactly what I set out to do in terms of making a difference," she said.

SUCCEEDING AGAINST THE ODDS

Antónette Colón . . .

CURRENT JOB:

Tax Compliance Consultant,
Arthur Andersen, LLP
(Hartford, Connecticut)

CAREER HIGHLIGHTS:

Enduring a childhood fraught with poverty and parental abuse, Antónette Colón learned, as early as the sixth grade, that the key to a promising future was a good education. Obtaining an education and achieving career satisfaction were not easy, but Antónette's tenacious desire to succeed, coupled with support from teachers, mentors, and friends, has enabled her to succeed as a tax lawyer with the largest international public accounting firm in the world. Three years into her practice she says she is "happy, safe, and free."

Born in Philadelphia to a young mother who had come to the United States from Puerto Rico, Antónette Colón remembers traveling to Hartford, Connecticut, to settle into a public housing project with her mother and sister. They were to be reunited with her grandmother, who later emigrated to the United States and searched for the daughter and grandchildren who had preceded her to this country. However, Antónette's mother was soon remarried to a man who could not support the family and who also became abusive. Finally, in Antónette's senior year of high school, she and her younger sister were taken into a foster home by her high school history teacher, who took both children into his home because he did not want them to be separated.

Apart from her foster parents, Antónette owes much of her success to her sixth grade teacher, Mrs. Harris, who taught at the Mary Hooker School. Antónette remembers winning first prize in a spelling bee and being the lucky winner of a steak dinner hosted by her teacher at a local restaurant. On the night of the dinner, Mrs. Harris realized that she had left her wallet at home, so she stopped there with Antónette. Mrs. Harris invited Antónette into her home for a few moments. Antónette remembers that she had never before been inside a private home. At that moment the house seemed to her to be "glamorous, beautiful, and bright."

Impressed, Antónette asked, "How can I have a beautiful home like this?" Mrs. Harris answered, "The more schooling you have, the more money you can make. You can buy anything you want . . . a house, a car . . . anything." Antónette considers the events of this particular evening to have been the root of her success. Before that, she had no hopes, dreams, or goals. All of a sudden everything clicked. After that evening Antónette received "A's" in school. She realized that her "ticket" out of her environment was to get a good education. By her senior year, she was valedictorian of her A.I. Prince School class. She worked hard in high school and saved money for college by working in a grocery store as a cashier.

Antónette attended Hartford College for Women, where she obtained an associate's degree, before attending Smith College, where she graduated with a B.A. in May 1990. She majored in clinical psychology, aspiring to be a child psychologist, because she wanted to understand "why people do what they do to their kids." Later, Antónette decided to go to law school and enrolled in the University of Connecticut School of Law so she could become a child advocate and protect the rights of children.

The first year of law school was very difficult, and Antónette often thought of dropping out, but she did not. She had taken out a loan to attend law school and felt she had to finish, not only to pay back the loan but also because she didn't consider herself a quitter.

In the spring of her first year of law school, she interviewed with law firms through the Career Development Internship program at the University of Connecticut School of Law and was chosen for an internship beginning in the fall of her second year as a law clerk with Reid and Riege, P.C., in Hartford, Connecticut. The hiring partner, John D'Amico (a University of Connecticut School of Law graduate), took a personal interest in mentoring Antónette. He helped her with her résumé and cover letters and taught her about what employers look for. Holding mock interview sessions in their offices, he and Robert Mulé, a corporate attorney at the firm, helped Antónette hone her interview skills. She worked for Reid and Riege throughout her second year of law school, gaining valuable skills and practical professional experience.

Antónette also remembers several professors who helped her get through law school. As part of a special academic support program offered by the law school two weeks before classes started, Professor Carol Weisbrod taught Antónette how to brief a case. Professor Robert Whitman was her upperclass writing advisor, and Antónette also took three classes with him. Professor Whitman continues to encourage her to write articles and perhaps teach a class on "Accounting and the Law" someday.

Antónette has always loved numbers, and she enjoyed the tax and trust and estate courses she took in law school. She interviewed with Arthur Andersen when they came on campus during the fall of her third year and was hired.

Today Antónette loves to go to work in the morning. She finds her work atmosphere very professional and says that everyone in the office enjoys working together. Her day begins at 8:00 a.m. with client work for which she is responsible. She handles tax filing requirements as well as tax issues and opportunities that arise for her clients. She works regular hours (40) in the summer but may work 60 or more hours per week from February through April due to the tax filing season. Fortunately, Arthur Andersen offers an excellent vacation package, and Antónette is able to take time off in the summer and fall.

Her first year at Arthur Andersen was the most difficult because she had to learn tax accounting, tax practice, and procedures. She found that the tax courses in law school were helpful, especially corporate and federal taxation. She feels that it was also helpful to have taken two or three accounting courses outside of the context of law school.

In addition to her work, Antónette is actively involved in her community. She was a guest speaker at a recent A.I. Prince Tech graduation. She has also participated in their Career Day, explaining what a career in public accounting involves and what the law entails. Through Arthur Andersen, she has also done some pro bono work on tax returns for non-profit organizations.

Antónette's advice to law students is to research an employer thoroughly before going on an interview. When she interviewed with Arthur Andersen, she quoted their recruiting brochure in an interview. She said to the interviewer, "According to your brochure, you are looking for people who are visionaries. It also says that you take risks. Do you want to take a risk with me? I'm not in the top of the class, but I will work hard."

Antónette is now very happy. Her life is better because she is free from the poverty of her early years—and free to have hopes and dreams for the future. Ten years from now, she would like to be a manager at Arthur Andersen while balancing a family and a career.

WORK TIME, NOT FACE TIME

Anne Yates . . .

CURRENT JOB:

Specialist, Montana
Department of Natural
Resources and Conservation
(Helena, Montana)

CAREER HIGHLIGHTS:

Anne Yates excelled both
in law school and as an
undergraduate. Following law
school graduation, she worked
for two years at a large D.C.
firm and three years at a small
D.C. firm. While Anne thought
that the hours at the small
firm were more reasonable,
she found the environment
was not. She left behind the
fast pace and money of the
metropolitan city and headed
West to Montana where she
now works and lives.

Anne Yates is happy today—simply happy. But it wasn't always that way for Anne. Having grown up in Raleigh, North Carolina, she was afraid if she didn't go to law school she would end up working as the manager of a chain shoe store in the local mall. She really didn't know what else to do. So, she went to law school.

Intelligent, bright, hard-working, and attractive, Anne strikes observers as a person who could have whatever she wants. Her career game plan started out with a basic strategy: go to law school, work in Washington, D.C., for a couple of years, then move back to North Carolina. But, as they say, life is what happens to you while you're busy making other plans—and things don't always go the way you plan.

Law school and the legal career in Washington, D.C., progressed as scheduled. Anne excelled academically at the University of North Carolina Law School in Chapel Hill, where she graduated with honors, sat on the moot court, and served as executive editor of *The North Carolina Journal of Commercial Regulation and International Law*. She traveled all over the country interviewing with various firms and corporations but ultimately decided to return to D.C. after graduation to work at the firm where she had clerked the previous summer. "I was drawn to D.C.," she says.

Although Anne stayed at the major D.C. law firm for only two years, she admits that she received terrific training at the firm and that there is no place like a large law firm to gain that kind of exposure and experience. However, her large firm experience was short on responsibility and long on hours. Anne headed back to The George Washington University Law School for an LL.M. in Environmental Law and obtained a part-time position with a small firm specializing in energy and natural resources. After a year in the LL.M. program, she completed her course work and started working full-time for the same small D.C. firm.

While at the small firm, Anne worked on a pro bono case with a client located in Montana. As a result, she decided to vacation in Montana one spring. This trip sparked Anne's first thoughts of leaving D.C. and relocating to Montana. Two more trips over the next year and a half allowed her to explore Montana and investigate whether it was a place she could live and thrive.

Anne had meanwhile become disillusioned—with the politics of D.C., with the tight legal industry that she felt pigeon-holed everyone into micro-specialized areas of the law, and with some of the attorneys she had met whom she found less than ethical. While the small firm hours proved more appealing and permitted a more balanced lifestyle, the environment proved less than nurturing and supportive, both personally and professionally. She became frustrated with the city, the job, and the lack of legal opportunities.

Anne realized she couldn't leave the Washington area until she finished the thesis for her LL.M. For a couple of years she talked about Montana and investigated moving West. Thinking about moving and actually moving were two incredibly different things, however. Anne faced a variety of obstacles beyond completing her thesis as she considered moving West. She faced fear of the unknown and of living in a place with no friends; family apprehensions about her moving 2,000 miles away; and the challenge of saving money for the move—including her need to purchase a car for the trip.

In a nutshell, her plan was to "finish the thesis, acquire that last Christmas bonus, and quit." Anne says, "It's funny how everything worked out." Just as she had planned, she finished her thesis in the winter of 1994, quit her job with the small firm in January 1995, and packed up her belongings. She left Washington with no job offer. She sought a more relaxed, slower pace of life—something that seemed to her less superficial than the priorities of the metropolitan area. She was motivated too by the opportunity to participate in a variety of outdoor activities—though now, after spending her first full winter in Montana, she admits that "it is bloody cold."

Prior to leaving Washington, Anne learned of a job opening in Montana. She applied, believing that she had little chance coming from out of state. She interviewed in transit. Anne received her job offer within a few weeks of arriving in Colorado, where she stayed with her sister and planned to job hunt. "I was incredibly lucky," she explains. "Jobs in Montana are few and far between." Anne is now an attorney specialist with the State's Department of Natural Resources and Conservation, and she does, as she says, "anything and everything" that has to do with state water products—dams, reservoirs, irrigation projects, and hydroelectric power. She conducts legal work in a variety of areas—from environmental and insurance law to litigation, Native American, and construction law.

Anne thoroughly enjoys her job. Now engineers are her clients. Her work is not only interesting but also provides a great deal of autonomy and responsibility. She finds the amount of responsibility compared to what she had in D.C. to be "like night and day." Anne has a great, ethical, progressive boss. When asked what makes him progressive, she responded that "he treats me [a woman] as an equal. Humor is a regular part of the office atmosphere, and it is just a 'people place.' People are there to do the job, not to see how many hours they can stay there." Anne also enjoys the fact that the legal work is preventative. She troubleshoots potential problems instead of just putting out fires, as was her previous experience in her law firm jobs.

When asked about any disadvantages in her new job, Anne states, "It's not for everyone." Like with any government job, the trappings are not glamorous, the pay is relatively low, and there are numerous bureaucratic hoops through which one has to jump. In addition, not everyone likes living in a small town. But, for Anne, the greater responsibility and the greater opportunities for interaction with people more than outweigh any drawbacks.

When asked if she has any regrets, Anne said emphatically, "NONE." She admitted that her friends and parents are too far away, but she made a lifestyle choice, and it was a trade-off she was willing to make.

Anne's advice to anyone considering leaving a metropolitan area for a different lifestyle is "Do It!" She believes that people need to "find out what is important for them." She adds, "People thought I was nuts for wanting to leave Washington, but it was good for me. You can't get carried away with what other people think of you. We get so wrapped up in the day-to-day of our lives, that we don't take a look."

SELLING A WONDERFUL INTANGIBLE

Leslie Ostrander . . .

CURRENT JOB:

Executive Director, BOYS HOPE (Cincinnati, Ohio)

CAREER HIGHLIGHTS:

Leslie Ostrander believes her lawyering skills contribute tremendously to her effectiveness as Executive Director of BOYS HOPE. During law school she gained work experience in two very different environments—working both with a Tenant Information Project and as an intern for Christian Dior New York. Following law school she joined the legal staff of a major insurance company, and then worked for a small law firm. Today she taps her ability to work with both public and private sectors to further the goals of an organization that makes a real and lasting difference in the lives of the boys it serves.

"I want to work with people" is a response that career counselors advise interviewees to avoid. But for Leslie Ostrander, this well-worn phrase rings true. More important for Leslie is making a positive difference in the lives of others. As Executive Director of BOYS HOPE in Cincinnati, Ohio, Leslie now combines her people skills with her commitment to making a difference in the lives of others, and she believes her legal training and work experience are critical factors in her effectiveness.

As a student at the University of Cincinnati College of Law, Leslie worked with a Tenant Information Project that provided assistance to individuals who needed support and were not sure where to turn. In addition, during law school she actively sought out a very different internship experience: a summer in New York City working for Christian Dior New York. In this internship, she was exposed to all aspects of a business operation, including trademark and licensing matters, while working directly with the U.S. corporate president.

After her law school graduation in 1989, Leslie joined the legal staff of a major insurance company. It was here, working closely with a vice-president to support the daily activities of the office, that she began to develop expertise in finding solutions to corporate and employment issues. These beginning business skills strengthened those she had already gained while at Christian Dior. Following this corporate experience, Leslie honed her lawyering skills through work at a small law firm.

When Leslie interviewed for her current position, the interviewer asked what she would bring to the organization. "What sold them on me," comments Leslie, "is that I was honest in saying that BOYS HOPE is a real opportunity for me." BOYS HOPE makes a real difference for a group of young boys by providing a home setting and academic expectations that permanently improve their lives. The position of Executive Director emphasizes Leslie's skills as a "people person." "I can talk to anybody," she says. "In this position, I am constantly called upon to make presentations on behalf of BOYS HOPE."

But "people skills" are only part of the equation. "My goal is to take the organization to a more effective and efficient level because of my lawyering skills," Leslie explains. She has done just that by moving BOYS HOPE from the red to the black in a mere 2 1/2 years. "I had handled my own work as an attorney, budgeting my time and balancing client needs," Leslie states. "In a business that truly makes a difference, the product is the best intangible—and one that I find very easy to promote." She feels strongly that "a job is an opportunity to get where you want to go" and adds, "My skills can be best applied in my position at BOYS HOPE."

As Executive Director of a non-profit agency, Leslie depends on the support of local corporations and influential members of the community. She is consistently in the position of having to ask for funding and for fundraising ideas. The BOYS HOPE Catalog provides an example of her fundraising creativity. The catalog offers information on "some of the items necessary to successfully raise a teenage boy" and details exactly how much those items cost—from milk money to birthday parties. Readers can thus "shop" for specific needs they wish to support.

Leslie enjoys the varied responsibilities involved in her role, but she also understands the importance of maintaining her focus. "Flexibility is truly a motivator for me," she says. "I work with people to develop and administer scholarships for our boys. We encourage volunteers on our board, and it is my responsibility to maximize their role. I organize fundraisers that are specific to a need. I believe that I have a lot of self-discipline as well as the expectation that I will succeed. For a child to succeed at BOYS HOPE, he must have a strong internal commitment. I feel that I must do the same. Seeing the vision is a good way to begin." Leslie believes that the success of BOYS HOPE depends upon a "consistent pattern of volunteer, social service activities."

Her current goal is to gain grant money for a "Girls Hope" that would enable her organization to expand its reach into the community. Leslie is involved in strategic planning with her board to establish a financial plan. Working with volunteers can be a challenge, but Leslie notes, "There are so many who are truly dedicated to supporting BOYS HOPE that I feel encouraged to continue to work closely with them to develop new ideas." Many years ago, Leslie felt strongly that there was a way to combine her legal education with her commitment to working with people to effect and support change. Today Leslie finds that her position at BOYS HOPE enables her to use a wide variety of the skills she learned at the University of Cincinnati College of Law. She is comfortable working with powerful people because of her experience at Christian Dior and at the large national insurance company where she spent her first year after law school—and just because of the law school/legal experience. She also knows that she has a wonderful intangible to sell when she talks about the children involved with BOYS HOPE.

A Publishing Entrepreneur

Tamara Traeder . . .

<u>Current Job</u>:

President of Circulus
Publishing Group, Inc., and
Publisher, PageMill Press
(Berkeley, California)

<u>Career Highlights</u>:

Tamara Traeder comes from an entrepreneurial family. After law school she worked in the San Francisco office of a large law firm for three years and then in a smaller startup San Francisco office of another firm for four more years before deciding to become an entrepreneur herself. She bought into PageMill Press, a small publishing company that specializes in holistic topics and psychology. Tamara is now not only a successful publisher but also a successful author.

Like most lawyers, Tamara Traeder loves reading, writing, and books. However, unlike most attorneys, Tamara followed these interests into a new career path. Tamara's desire for more creativity in a more collaborative field led her into the world of publishing—and to her current position as President of Circulus Publishing Group, Inc., and Publisher of Pagemill Press in Berkeley, California.

Tamara obtained her J.D. at the University of Virginia, then decided to go into business law because she came from an entrepreneurial family. Following graduation in 1985, she worked in the San Francisco office of a large law firm. In 1988, Tamara accepted a position with another large law firm that had established a small startup office in San Francisco, allowing her broader practice areas and more responsibility.

Although Tamara stayed at this firm until 1992, she had thought about work alternatives since her second year of practice. The rational part of Tamara's nature had told her not to leave law because she "hadn't given it enough of a chance." Yet she felt stifled and longed for more creativity in her work. "With work consuming all my time," notes Tamara, "I found it difficult to grow as a multi-dimensional person."

In her sixth year of practice, Tamara began to consider the idea of working in publishing, which was suggested by a friend who knew Tamara loved books. She applied for and was accepted by an educational publishing program but was hesitant to take the time off from work or to explain the six-week absence necessary for the program. Tamara then enrolled in a course that was part of the University of California at Berkeley's publishing program. She initially took the course with the idea of working as an inhouse lawyer at a publishing company. Tamara became friends with her instructor, who then introduced her to others involved in the publishing industry. She was amazed by the mindset and the helpfulness of these people. "There is not a lot of money to be made in small publishing," she comments, "so the people involved love it or leave it."

Tamara next took a course on legal issues in publishing. Once again she made a positive connection with the instructor. When Tamara finally decided she wanted to leave her firm at the end of 1992, she began to do contract legal work for this instructor—providing a source of income that allowed her to quit full-time practice. Tamara had also saved some money—she says it is important to have a financial reserve—and had developed plans to buy into a small publishing company.

After seven years of legal practice, during which her career path was slowly and methodically evolving, Tamara was ready for more rapid changes. Within two months, she had sold her house in San Francisco, moved to Berkeley, quit her law firm job, and bought into a small publishing company named PageMill Press, which specializes in books on holistic topics and psychology. "I knew I didn't want to practice law full-time for the rest of my life," says Tamara, "and when the opportunity to buy into the Press arose, I had the means to pursue it and also had the intuitive feeling that I needed to make this change in order to maintain balance in my life."

However, when Tamara started at PageMill, she still didn't know as much as she wanted about her new specialty, so she took more courses in the editorial and marketing aspects of publishing. At the same time, she was busy dealing with the kinds of business issues she did know, this time in the context of publishing, such as tax status and contracts. Once Tamara learned a bit more, she became involved in soliciting and reading manuscripts, marketing, and dealing with authors and their representatives. She has continued to do legal work relating to her own business.

Tamara likes the variety inherent in working in a small business. She finds publishing to be creative and interesting, whether she is deciding marketing strategies or formulating book ideas. She likes working with people in cooperative ventures. Tamara now thinks in terms of "how can we work together to achieve a common goal" rather than of "us against them." She finds that people in publishing tend to be more creative and more open to new ideas than many corporate lawyers. However, Tamara believes lawyers are well-suited to working within small businesses because they are trained to problem solve and to get things done.

Tamara advises those who are agonizing over a potential job or career change to "listen to your gut and pay attention to what feels right for you—and don't be swayed by other people's opinions because everyone will tell you not to take risks." She also suggests taking "relevant courses to get information on day-to-day issues. Because it's a friendly industry," she adds, "it is okay to call publishing houses and ask for information."

According to Tamara, "If you want to make a move into the publishing field, you need to save money before making the change in order to allow yourself a bit of financial freedom." Tamara illustrates her point by noting, "I didn't draw a regular salary from PageMill Press for three years—in publishing, there is a long lead time to get a payback from a developing book."

As a publisher, Tamara now drafts publishing agreements with authors ("having a legal background is certainly helpful here," she says). And, with her partners, she markets books for reviews and publicity, assists authors with book ideas and structure, handles logistics and office work, deals with distributors and printers, and generally does whatever else needs to be done.

There are currently three partners in PageMill Press. One partner had her own publishing company, which was incorporated into one entity with PageMill Press in 1995. That entity is called Circulus Publishing Group, Inc. As a result, the press has two imprints—Wildcat Canyon Press as well as PageMill Press. At the time Tamara was interviewed for this book, the combined entity had 13 books in various stages of development or already in distribution. In fact, one of the books, titled *Girlfriends*, was co-authored by Tamara with Carmen Berry. It has been successfully marketed throughout the U.S., and Tamara has just finished a national book tour, including network television and radio interviews. Two hundred and fifty thousand copies of *Girlfriends* have already been printed, with additional runs projected. In addition, Tamara and Carmen published a sequel in late 1996 called *The Girlfriends Keepsake Book*.

Pretty heady stuff for someone previously longing for more creativity in her work. For others interested in learning more about the publishing field, Tamara recommends *Publishers Weekly* magazine, which she calls the "bible of publishing," and *Small Press* magazine. In addition, she suggests that the Publishers' Marketing Association can help small publishers learn about the industry and about marketing—and that many major cities have local publishing associations which can be located through local bookstores.

CREATIVE PROBLEM SOLVER FINDS A CORPORATE NICHE

Gabrielle Hager . . .

CURRENT JOB:

Managing Attorney,
Environmental Litigation,
Electric Insurance Company
(Beverly, Massachusetts)

CAREER HIGHLIGHTS:

Four years of law firm real estate and environmental law practice provided Gabrielle with an excellent foundation for her transition into the corporate world. In her current position, Gabrielle both manages cases and tracks national trends. Her talents for thinking strategically and globally are crucial to her success as a corporate lawyer. Gabrielle also credits her achievements to her ability to see cases as opportunities for creative problem solving rather than as battles.

As an attorney who manages environmental litigation for the Electric Insurance Company, Gabrielle Hager not only manages specific cases but also forecasts and tracks national trends and thinks about global solutions and litigation prevention strategies. The company's primary policy holder is a Fortune 5 company for which Gabrielle focuses on "toxic tort" litigation.

When Gabrielle attended law school at Northwestern University School of Law, she didn't know exactly what type of law she wanted to practice, but she knew she wanted to be a litigator. She also wanted to get involved in the public sector, either in international diplomacy or politics. Her current job is "amazingly political," she says, because she deals with issues that "people read about in the newspapers." Asbestos litigation is one of the areas in which she works. It is such a complex area with so many plaintiffs that the courts cannot handle the burden of litigation by themselves and have set up commissions to look at the problems. These commissions involve the

Congress, the Judiciary, industry and the AFL-CIO, and others. Everyone has to agree on a solution, so there is a lot of lobbying involved, as well as much exchanging of political favors.

Although Gabrielle found law school to be a real struggle, she managed to obtain fantastic summer positions and a great first job after graduation. She parlayed her paralegal experience at Covington & Burling in Washington, D.C., and her winning personality into summer associate positions with two well-respected firms: Howrey & Simon in Washington, D.C., and Fine & Ambrogne in Boston. Her first job out of law school was as an associate with Gaston & Snow, a large law firm in Boston, where she practiced in the areas of real estate litigation and environmental litigation. This job prepared her well for her current position. Real estate was booming in Boston and New England, and she got involved in major disputes between developers, lenders, architects, tenants, and public finance agencies.

The state courts' motion practice system gave Gabrielle great practical experience and training. The courts held a motion call every morning from 10:00 a.m. until noon. Junior associates were sent to make these motion calls any time there was a motion to be argued on a case on which they were working. Since there was no set time for their motion to be heard, they would often hear many motions argued before they argued their own. This exposed junior associates to different lawyering styles while also allowing them to gain experience.

The highlight of Gabrielle's four years at the law firm was a case where she represented a French businessman in a visitation case. When his ex-wife found out that he was gay, she did not want to send their son to visit him in France, as the custody order decreed. In explaining why she enjoyed the case immensely, Gabrielle comments, "I had direct contact with the client, and the ownership of the case was entirely mine. I was so excited about this case that I went out of my mind with preparation. I kept thinking of different motions and ways to approach the case." Opposing counsel on the case was a partner with a major Boston law firm. He was so impressed by Gabrielle's performance that he offered her a job at the conclusion of the case.

Gabrielle found her transition from law firm to corporation to be an easy one because she likes to deal with litigation at a global level and she prefers managing cases and devising strategies to actually carrying out all of the details of litigation, such as preparing interrogatories and taking depositions. She also enjoys being able to speak in a straightforward manner to business people and not having to talk legalese.

Gabrielle admits that her greatest weakness as a lawyer is in technical thinking, which she found particularly difficult when she had to rotate through the corporate and real estate departments at Gaston & Snow. What carried her through was being extremely organized. In her position at EIC, Gabrielle doesn't have to be such a strong technical lawyer. What is more important is her ability to think strategically and globally. This is particularly important since EIC's policy holders have litigation nation-wide on very similar issues. Gabrielle attributes her success to her abili-ty to be a creative problem solver and to the fact that she does not view every case as a battle.

Gabrielle's organizational skills have also been crucial to her success at EIC. After the birth of a child in 1993, she negotiated with EIC to do her full-time job in four days a week instead of five. This has meant working long hours, giving up lunch hours, and maintaining lots of energy, but it has allowed Gabrielle to spend more time with her three sons, who are now 12 years old, 3 years old, and 6 months old. Gabrielle notes that one of the difficulties she has encountered at work has been her pregnancies because "people treat you like an alien when you're pregnant."

The attorney whom Gabrielle most admires has great style as a lawyer. "She is an amazing litigator who gets her way and gets the settlements she wants without making an enemy," Gabrielle comments. This ability is invaluable in environmental litigation because there is a great deal of repeat business with the same opposing counsel. If an attorney makes an enemy, she or he may not be able to settle as easily with that attorney in the future. "This is a nice quality that many women lawyers have," notes Gabrielle. "Instead of getting caught in the war, they think out of the box about how to reach the desired end."

Gabrielle thinks about teaching environmental law at a prep school or college some day. She loves teaching and young people and likes making presentations to others. What most interests her is the political aspects and public policy consequences of environmental law and the interesting issues that arise from that interplay.

An Unending Quest for Learning

Melanie McCall . . .

CURRENT JOB:

Senior Associate, JHTM &
Associates, Facilities
Engineers (Costa Mesa,
California)

CAREER HIGHLIGHTS:

Before entering law school,
Melanie McCall had already
written legislation for a
Southern California municipality; provided technical and
marketing consultation for the
architectural and engineering
fields; and worked for the
Chairman of the House Budget
Committee at the Ohio House
of Representatives. After graduating in the top 10% of her
law school class, she spent
two years learning the ropes of
real estate and transactional
law at an international law
firm in Los Angeles. Her colleagues from the engineering
field, however, followed her
tracks—and stellar reputation—and eventually lured her
back into consulting. Now,
Melanie combines her legal
skills and technical interests
in a highly satisfying career.

Melanie McCall's interest in pursuing a law career was sparked
during undergraduate school, but
"became dormant," she says, when
she moved from Ohio to California
soon after graduating from the
University of Cincinnati with a
communications degree. For the
next six years, she developed
expertise in administering public
relations and marketing programs
for engineering and architectural
consulting firms. From the production of press releases to market
research to editing technical
reports on redevelopment and public finance, she managed to explore
just about every nook and cranny
the job had to offer her.

Melanie finally reached a point,
however, when she was ready to do
more. She also realized that she still
had a law degree to pursue—and
that it was now or never.

At the start of law school, she
was intrigued with criminal and
civil rights law. It wasn't long
before those interests changed.
Having a strong background in
engineering and land development, Melanie naturally gravitated
toward real estate.

She graduated with top marks
from Loyola Law School in Los

Angeles. With an impressive background of leadership, solid work experience, and a relaxed, friendly personality—the qualities of an excellent team player—Melanie had no trouble landing a first-year associate job at Whitman Breed Abbott & Morgan.

At the firm, Melanie first got her feet wet working in the litigation department. In addition to researching and drafting court documents, she attended a number of court hearings. Eventually, she moved to the corporate department, where she felt very much at home practicing real estate law.

Through this experience, Melanie recognized the biggest difference between litigation and transactional work: In corporate she was putting together deals. Litigation takes place once the deal has fallen apart and lawyers must then make a case on one side of it. She found her preference was for saving relationships through transactional work rather than for dealing with them once they fell apart. In addition, since moving to California, Melanie had always been involved in real estate. "In this area," she comments, "you deal with land, buildings, and a lot of requirements. Being detail-oriented, that has always appealed to me."

While ultimately opting for transactional work, Melanie regards her time in litigation as valuable experience. It forced her to be more careful as a transactional attorney because she understood that "just one word can change the intent of an agreement or a key provision."

With her multiple talents and newly acquired legal training, it is not a surprise that Melanie was persistently sought after by engineering colleagues with whom she had worked before law school.

Steve Bucknam, vice-president of IWA Engineers in Fountain Valley, California, remembers meeting Melanie 10 years ago when he retained her consulting services. "As marketing director, she always impressed me with her innovative ideas and creative thinking. By the time she decided to go to law school, she had become invaluable to me. Her positive personality was my spark plug."

For Melanie, the opportunity to return to engineering consulting has resulted in finding a true niche for herself. Establishing business contacts before attending law school—and maintaining those relationships—had a lot to do with her move back to the field. Steve remarks that while Melanie is not practicing law *per se*, her added legal background provides the important missing link in creating an effective management team, a trend he feels many businesses are following.

Many of their projects, for example, require constant communication with the city attorney, who is not always readily accessible. Having Melanie on board lessens that anxiety. According to Steve, she is already very instrumental in a current water project, which is cutting new ground and could become a model for other cities in Southern California.

On other occasions, Melanie drafts contract specifications for construction projects where she works closely with the public agency legal counsel and general contractors ensuring compliance with the intricacies of public contract codes. When doing airport work, she must have knowledge of FAA requirements; in other cases, she deals with infrastructure issues such as roads and utilities.

Technical consulting has exposed Melanie to a variety of areas where learning something new is the day's agenda. "Another interesting area of my job is on the policy level," she notes. "We do a lot of preliminary analysis such as potential annexations by a city or a water district."

Melanie's consulting work also satisfies the social side of her personality. She has the opportunity for constant client contact, a part of her job she really enjoys—and something she missed while at the law firm. A typical week for Melanie at JHTM includes three to four meetings out of the office with clients and other consultants.

Staying abreast of what's going on in the legal field is a priority for Melanie. She remains active in local and state bar associations, which her firm supports. Programs on environmental law help keep her informed on topics such as air and water quality.

Melanie, recently married, unhesitatingly contends that her alternative career move has not only worked out for her professionally but on a personal level, too. Her definition of success is finding the balance between career and financial needs, time demands, and personal life. "For some of my law school classmates, the professional side needs to be dominant; for others, it's less so. Although the decision to switch careers was a big one, I know it was right for me."

A Career on the Cutting Edge

Cathy E. Shore-Sirotin. . . .

Current Job:

Associate at Hall Dickler Kent Friedman & Wood LLP (New York City)

Career Highlights:

Cathy Shore-Sirotin helps clients navigate the legal intricacies of communications, advertising, and trademark law. She has defended the trademark rights of large global companies as well as those of much smaller startup companies engaged in launching new products and services. An especially memorable career highlight was being part of the "winning team" representing various NFL players and the NFL Players Association in litigation vs. the NFL—and assisting in negotiating and drafting the current NFL collective bargaining agreement that resulted from the litigation.

If you've ever wondered what stops advertisers from making outrageous claims about their products, meet Cathy Shore-Sirotin. Reviewing commercial scripts and other advertising copy for legal acceptability, Cathy performs a vital quality control check that allows advertisers and their advertising agencies to fulfill one of their primary purposes: to educate the public. In the fast-paced world of advertising, this can sometimes mean being contacted by a client from a commercial "shoot" in progress for an on-the-spot consultation. However, it may be the highspeed fun of advertising that led Cathy to develop a specialty in advertising, trademark, and communications law in the first place.

As a psychology major at the University of Pennsylvania, Cathy began dabbling in marketing courses. Finding a lot of crossover between the two fields, she eventually earned both a B.A. in psychology and a B.S. in marketing from the Wharton School. Working at a small advertising agency during college provided a positive, hands-on introduction to the field. "It seemed very interesting to me," Cathy remembers. "It was something I could relate to because, like everyone else,

I watched commercials on television; it just seemed exciting and the people who worked in advertising seemed to enjoy their work."

Five years after graduation, Cathy had worked her way up to a Marketing Manager position at Citicorp and was about to be promoted to Assistant Vice-President when she paused to reconsider her career path. Her job now entailed more corporate strategic planning than marketing or advertising, a direction not entirely in keeping with Cathy's true interests. There was also another consideration: a longheld thought of attending law school one day kept nagging at Cathy—maybe now was the right time. The daughter of a successful named partner at a prestigious midsize firm, Cathy believes she rebelled against attending law school right out of college because, at the time, it seemed more her family's plan than her own. Thus, in 1988, Cathy earned an M.B.A. in marketing at N.Y.U.'s Graduate School of Business (now the Stern School), which she attended at night. Now, after having proved herself a success in her own way, Cathy was ready to pursue her law school dream.

She garnered honors during her career at Fordham University School of Law. Cathy graduated in 1990 in the top 10% of the class, was a member of the moot court board, and held an editorial position on the then newly formed Intellectual Property, Media and Entertainment Law Journal. She went on to clerk for a federal judge in California after graduation, and a year later began work as a trade regulation/litigation associate at Weil, Gotshal & Manges, LLP, in New York.

At Weil, most of Cathy's time was devoted to antitrust matters, but, through her own initiative, she sought and gained experience in advertising, trademark, copyright, sports, and unfair competition law. It was while working on an advertising case that Cathy first came in contact with the attorneys at Hall Dickler Kent Friedman & Wood LLP, a 70+attorney, New York-based law firm known nationally for its advertising law expertise. After two years at Weil, Cathy believed she would have to move on if she wished to develop further expertise in advertising law because this practice area was somewhat limited at Weil. In a sense, Cathy had come full circle when she joined Hall Dickler as an advertising associate in 1992. At Citicorp she had presented marketing materials to the legal department for review; now at Hall Dickler Cathy performs this task herself.

Cathy's daily activities at Hall Dickler can range from copy review for various consumer products and promotions to trademark clearance and registration to the negotiation and drafting of talent, agency/advertiser, licensing, and sponsorship agreements. Although Cathy says no day is "typical," a good portion of each is spent advising clients on these matters. Having an M.B.A. in addition to a J.D. is helpful, Cathy finds, as law becomes more business-oriented, and as she interacts frequently with clients—or general counsel for various clients—who have a business background. Being "tenacious," as a law professor once described Cathy, is also helpful in obtaining the full story from clients. Understandably, clients will often present information in a way that is most favorable to them, Cathy says. Persistence is needed to bring all the facts of a case to light and to be able to truly represent clients to their best advantage.

Common pitfalls Cathy helps advertisers avoid before their promotional material reaches the public include overstating the claims for their product and committing copyright and trademark infringement. Cutting-edge issues within the field include the application of trademark and advertising law to the Internet in general and, most notably, the use of domain names on the Internet. Cathy explains, "Trademark rights are territorial, so one company can own a mark in the U.S. and another company can own it in France, for example. Prior to the Internet, they could very easily be distinct markets." But once companies are on the Internet, who has ownership? As advertising reaches the Net, which country's advertising laws regulate it? Domain names refer to a company's unique address on the World Wide Web. Cathy illuminates this issue: "The problem is that more than one company can normally have rights to the same trademark as long as both are used for totally different goods. An example would be Cadillac, since both Cadillac dog food and Cadillac cars exist. However, the Internet domain name *Cadillac.com* can only refer to one company."

While Cathy helps clients navigate the legal intricacies of communications law on the Internet, her personal life has become more complex since the birth of her son, Maxwell, in August 1995. Maxwell has necessitated bringing the art of organization and efficiency to even higher levels than the obviously organized and efficient Cathy had already achieved. A supportive husband who, as principal in his own firm, has a work schedule that is somewhat more flexible than Cathy's helps make it all possible.

Attempting to carve out a career in a field as coveted and as limited as advertising and trademark law proves to be a daunting task for most. That Cathy Shore-Sirotin has succeeded is testament to her ability in undertaking planned risks as well as to her unique talents and determination.

Creating Solutions in a Downsized Market

Jodi L. Nadler & Beth E. Fleischer . . .

Current Jobs:

Principals and Founders of Law Pros Legal Placement Services, Inc. (Livingston, New Jersey)

Career Highlights:

Jodi Nadler and Beth Fleischer graduated from law school in 1993, at the peak of an economic downturn in the legal market. Their stories might have been like those of so many other frustrated graduates of the time, but Jodi and Beth turned the tables by tapping their frustrations—and their skills and entrepreneurial spirit—to found Law Pros, one of the most successful new women-owned and operated businesses in the Northeast. Through Law Pros, Jodi and Beth help law firms and corporations that are seeking talented attorneys as well as assisting attorneys who are seeking temporary and permanent work.

Entrepreneurs Jodi Nadler and Beth Fleischer have combined their legal degrees with an entrepreneurial spirit to help young attorneys who are seeking their first postgraduate legal positions and experienced attorneys who want to explore new practice areas or reenter the job market. Along the way, Beth and Jodi have emerged as prominent authors and spokeswomen who are in great demand by the media for their insight into the employment market and their success as innovative female entrepreneurs.

Jodi was raised in Montville, New Jersey, and Beth was raised in Livingston, New Jersey. Jodi received her B.A. from Rutgers College, New Brunswick, and her J.D. from George Washington University School of Law in Washington, D.C. She is admitted to the Bars of New Jersey and New York. Beth received her B.A. from the University of Delaware and her J.D. from Widener University School of Law in Wilmington, Delaware. She is admitted to the Bars of New Jersey and Pennsylvania.

Both women had been driven

achievers throughout childhood, college, and law school, and yet, completion of their law degrees did not initially bring fortune or exciting career paths their way.

Jodi recalls that, after her graduation from George Washington University, the downsizing of many law firms made obtaining entry-level law firm positions difficult. Jodi and Beth had the "good fortune" of graduating from law school in 1993, near the peak of a downturn in the legal market. Their story is like many others of this time period, but their solution was unique and remains inspiring. Highly motivated by intelligence, grit, determination, and law school debt, they saw their own expectations spiral downward as their promising job offers in law firms were reneged due to budget constraints. "We knew the firms were sincerely battling economic downturn," they comment, "but it hurt nonetheless."

Frustrated by having to compete with more experienced attorneys for a dearth of entry-level associate positions, Jodi and Beth—who did not yet know each other—each decided to turn to temporary legal work. In so doing, they gained partnership possibilities beyond their dreams. While working as temporary personnel in a large in-house corporate legal department, Jodi and Beth found themselves doing the type of transactional work many attorneys dream of. However, despite positive feedback, frustration struck again. They were denied opportunities to apply for full-time employment because of the company's policy of hiring only those attorneys with at least four to six years of prior law firm experience. A catch-22. Yet, Beth and Jodi persevered.

While working as temporary professionals they had met and become not only colleagues but also good friends. Together they shared their experiences and their insights into the challenges being faced by many law school graduates during the economic downturn in the legal market. Their friendship soon turned into a partnership. The two discussed their thoughts, goals, and frustrations regarding the legal market and found that they shared a common belief that temporary services for legal professionals were a necessary and viable alternative. Together they conducted extensive market research and surveyed the existing climate. Then they co-founded Law Pros.

Law Pros specializes in assisting members of the legal community to increase their staffing and productivity through exceptional attorney and paralegal staffing solutions. Jodi and Beth stress the importance of the fact that Law Pros is owned and managed by attorneys. They also stress their distinctive candidate recruitment and selection process and the efficiency for employers through savings of time and money. For temporary placements, Law Pros offers new or experienced attorneys to businesses that need a specific legal service but don't wish to add permanent personnel at the time. For the temporary employees, there are sensitive and caring professionals in Jodi and Beth to offer two badly needed commodities . . . experience and a paycheck!

Both Beth and Jodi are actively involved with the American Bar Association, the New Jersey State Bar Association, and their county bar associations. They participate in the Legal Assistants Association of New Jersey, the New Jersey Association of Temporary Services, the National Association of Temporary Staffing and Services, the National Association of Personnel Services, the National Association of Legal Search Consultants, and the Society of Human Resource Management, and they serve as associate members of the Board of Directors of the New Jersey Staffing Association.

Beth and Jodi are also actively involved in community affairs. They are members of and serve on the Board of Trustees as Co-Vice-Presidents of Government Affairs and Legislation for the Essex County Chapter of the New Jersey Association of Women Business Owners. They are in demand as authors and guest lecturers, have been featured on the nationally syndicated cable television show Celebrity Sports and Entertainment, and have been interviewed by the *New Jersey Law Journal, New Jersey Lawyer*, the *Star Ledger*, and *Corporate Counsel* magazine.

Jodi and Beth remain at the forefront of the intensely competitive Northeast temporary and permanent legal markets because of their professionalism and their commitment to both of the constituencies they represent—legal employers and professional staff candidates. Their own hands-on knowledge of the legal profession and their experiences in a tighter economic climate help Beth and Jodi to genuinely empathize with the frustrations facing attorneys who are seeking both temporary and permanent professional employment and with the staggering workloads being experienced by the downsized staffs of corporations and law firms.

Jodi and Beth truly put their hearts and souls into their business. They are justifiably proud to be owners of a state-certified Women Business Enterprise. They see their role as one of providing a badly needed solution to the problems the legal community has recently experienced. And they draw from their own wealth of experience to leave in their wake satisfied employer clients, recruits, and professional temporary employees who feel that they have been privileged to be treated to the height of dignity and professionalism by Jodi Nadler and Beth Fleischer. Through their professional staffing service these two women are clearly making a permanent impact on the needs of the legal community.

BALANCING THE MANY "SPOKES" OF LIFE

Michael Levelle . . .

CURRENT JOB:

Attorney, Sussman Shank
Wapnick Caplan & Stiles LLP
(Portland, Oregon)

CAREER HIGHLIGHTS:

Michael Levelle is a principle-driven individual. He possesses an unusual combination of training and experience in social work and law, as well as expertise in the study of social forces. His background, which includes service in Vietnam, provides him with a unique perspective of the law—and of life. Not content to settle for career "satisfaction," this husband and father of five has found fulfillment by maintaining a balance in the "spokes on the wheel" of his multi-faceted life.

The Vietnam War played a major role in shaping Michael Levelle's career. He served in Vietnam from 1971-1972. Upon returning, Michael was, in his own words, "a very typical Vietnam vet. I was alienated both socially and politically," he says. "I was disillusioned and had no personal focus or direction *per se*. I worked, and I dreamed of buying land in Montana and living a 'back to nature' life."

From 1972 to 1987, Michael traveled and worked in Hawaii and Colorado, doing stints as a carpenter, waiter, and truck driver. By 1983, he was becoming more reflective and wondering, "Is this what I want to do for the next 20 years of my life?" Deciding to return to school, he earned his bachelor's degree at night while working during the day.

Michael developed an interest in social work and did volunteer work as a peer counselor with Vietnam veterans. During his social work practicum in college, he worked in a law office, training people to become guardians ad litem. "I was training nonlegal persons to represent children who had come in contact with the legal system, usually as victims of abuse," Michael explains. A guardian ad litem does not serve in a legal capacity but is rather a source of support and nonlegal advocacy.

Through the practicum Michael received exposure to the ways legal skills and training could benefit society. A dream he had as a young adolescent was resurrected also—to become a lawyer. As a youth, he was dissuaded from that dream. "A law career was not a part of the 'world view' for many African-Americans in the mid-1960s," Michael recalls. "There was not as much consciousness of the need for diversity in the legal profession." Even his family discouraged him from pursuing law, perhaps wanting to shield him, he believes, from inevitable disappointment.

Twenty years later, the dream resurfaced. Michael's practicum gave him exposure to the field of law and, he adds, "the experience to gauge whether I really wanted to do it." He decided to attend law school and work with children in a legal capacity.

Although Michael was interested in remaining in his native Montana, he also yearned for the Pacific Northwest, which he had loved during his travels. "I was striving to be challenged by the practice of law," Michael comments. "I was not sure I would have been challenged as much practicing in Montana, given my interest in social issues and the relatively rural area surrounding Missoula." He was attracted to the more urban areas of Portland and Seattle and chose Willamette University College of Law, which offered him a scholarship.

Michael says of law school, "It was, overall, a very positive experience. But the study of law creates a sometimes hostile environment for minority students. I was an African-American in a predominantly white environment. A student of color has to deal with issues of racism in law school while studying how discriminatory the law is and was 50 or 100 years ago—for example, the way that rationalizations were created to support specific discriminatory rulings of the law. You recognize the emotional impact those issues have on you as a person, and yet as a law student you still have to study and pass exams in a way that satisfies professors."

Michael believes that the social context of the legal profession is changing irrevocably. "Discrimination still exists in all professions; it just gets more subtle," he says. "Things are changing. It [the workplace] is becoming more volatile. You used to have different rules for blacks and whites working together. Now, with increased diversity in the workplace and the empowerment among all groups, there's discomfort—there is an awareness of different world views all operating in the same context. That creates new social rules. For example, in Montana, Native American tribes are sending their children to law school, and they return and practice law on behalf of the Indian Nations. That creates changes in tribal rights and in the relationship between the tribes and the U.S. government." African-Americans are gradually gaining access to "partner status" in medium to large private law firms. These positions enable them to influence firm policy from the inside, not just the outside. Michael's social work training and experience give him a unique perspective on the varying "world views" among racial and ethnic groups—and on how those views are applied to the law. "A 'world view,' " he says, "creates the social context within which laws are created and law is practiced."

The law firm of Sussman Shank Wapnick Caplan & Stiles LLP, where Michael now practices, is a 22-attorney firm that serves a broad range of clients from individuals to family businesses and public corporations. Michael works mainly with elderly clients and representing fiduciaries such as conservators, guardians, and trustees. Ironically, he became interested in his practice area while working as a labor lawyer representing union clients. As a junior lawyer he would freqently be given the assignment of preparing estate plans for individual union members. He loved working in the area, so he decided to stick with it. His work is at the opposite end of the age spectrum from the practice he had initially envisioned for himself.

Michael's motivation stems from his desire to create change. "I am given a unique opportunity as an officer of the court to effect change," he explains. "I do have power." He admires lawyers who, in his words, have "the ability to listen using active listening skills, which I gained as a social worker. You must not only focus on clients' rights but also on their needs." He also admires the ability to work hard at a high energy level—and dedication to the pursuit of goodness. "I see lawyers dedicate their skills to creating a lot of good in the world," he comments.

One challenge facing all lawyers is what Michael calls an "ego" issue involved in practicing law. He explains, "Lawyers have to have a strong ego to be successful, but the flip side is that they must not allow that ego to get in the way. The strong ego is necessary to deal with failing and feeling unsuccessful . . . when you don't achieve all you want to." He believes that for some lawyers strong egos, untempered, become detriments to their careers.

Michael has a strong sense of what makes lawyers successful. "Part of the ability to be a successful attorney is time," he says. "The longer you practice, the better you get. I'm a much better lawyer and a much better person than I was five years ago. I have taken the unique opportunities that lawyers are exposed to and applied them to my own personal values. That makes me a more well-rounded person." Michael's success as a lawyer also depends on the principles that guide his personal life. "The study of law is easy. Living the rest of your life is the challenge," he comments. "It's not just learning to think like a lawyer, it's also learning how to be a person."

Those principles are intertwined with Michael's strong desire to live a balanced life. "Successful lawyers are able to balance their lives," he says. "In my social work background, we called it the 'wheel' concept—many spokes, each representing one facet of life. If spokes are missing, the whole wheel is affected. I have five children. I am very sensitive to the need to balance my career with my kids' needs for me to be there. Reading to my children at night, for example, is therapeutic for them and for me. It's successful and rewarding."

Michael's advice to those considering law is to continually reassess their career goals. "Be in touch with who you are as an individual," he advises. "What is the right path for others may not be right for you. In this profession, there's a lot of ego wrapped up in being successful. Lawyers get into a mindset of feeling like a failure if they leave the law. You need to have a 'touchstone,' a way of making assessments about whether you're happy. When you pursue a law career, your vision may change. You should allow it to."

Michael makes an important distinction between satisfaction and fulfillment in a career and cautions against merely settling for satisfaction: "Never hesitate, if you aren't happy, to find something else to do."

Michael has found the work that gives him fulfillment. He has the capacity to continually reassess his life, and the wherewithal to change when necessary. Many lawyers would envy that ability. It's a big part of what makes Michael Levelle a successful attorney and a successful human being.

AT THE HELM OF THE EPA

Carol M. Browner . . .

CURRENT JOB:

Administrator, U.S. Environmental Protection Agency (Washington, D.C.)

CAREER HIGHLIGHTS:

Following law school gradua-tion, Carol Browner went to work as General Counsel for the Government Operations Committee of the Florida House of Representatives. There former Governor Leroy Collins became her mentor and taught her to understand the challenge and necessity of writing a good law. Carol next moved to Washington, D.C., where she worked first for Citizen Action, a grassroots consumer group, and later in several Congressional posi-tions before returning to Florida as the Secretary of the Department of Environmental Protection for the state. In 1993, she was tapped by President Clinton to head the U.S. Environmental Protection Agency.

As the Administrator of the U.S. Environmental Protection Agency, Carol Browner's mission is to pro-mote public health by protecting our nation's air, water, and soil. Although she never dreamed she would one day hold the nation's top environmental post, Carol always planned to seek a career in public service—thanks to her father's strong influence. Carol's father grew up in Ireland and moved to the United States as a young man with nothing. He served in the Army dur-ing the Korean War and, as a result, the government helped him to finance his education and purchase his first home. He became a teacher in order to give something back to a country that he felt had given him so much. "My father taught me that I have a responsibility to give some-thing back," Carol explains. She adds, "Going to law school was my way to begin to fulfill that responsi-bility . . . a route to engaging in pub-lic service."

Although Carol attended the University of Florida College of Law at a time when there were few women law students and even fewer female role models, she enjoyed her law school experience and the intel-lectual challenges of studying law.

She especially enjoyed learning about the laws which guide our nation. Her desire to work in public service was furthered in law school through an internship at Legal Aid and through her work with the University of Florida's Center for Government Responsibility. Reflecting on her experience, she comments, "As an intern at Legal Aid, I worked with battered women and women in prison. I learned that representing people through individual cases can be very powerful. Through that experience, I began to develop an interest in using my legal knowledge on a larger scale . . . to improve the lives of many by seeking to change public policies."

Following graduation, Carol went to work as General Counsel for the Government Operations Committee of the Florida House of Representatives. While working for the Florida legislature, Carol had the opportunity to work with former Florida Governor Leroy Collins, whom she considers a significant mentor in her early career. Collins, who was retired, continued to advise legislators on how to craft legislation, and he and Carol had the opportunity to rewrite a law together. "He moved me to understand the challenge and necessity of writing a good law," Carol comments.

Carol's next career move took her to Washington, D.C., to work for Citizen Action, a grassroots consumer group, and later as the Chief Legislative Aid for Environmental Issues to then-Senator Lawton Chiles. During this time, Carol was involved in several environmental challenges facing Florida . . . including a land swap to protect the areas around the Everglades and the Pinhook Area Swamp and a federal moratorium on oil drilling off the Florida Keys. When Chiles left the Senate in 1988, Carol served as Counsel to the Senate Committee on Energy and Natural Resources—and as Legislative Director to then-Senator Al Gore. From 1991 to 1993, she served as Secretary of the Department of Environmental Protection for the State of Florida and earned praise for building innovative partnerships to protect public health while also promoting economic growth.

In her current role as administrator of the EPA, Carol finds her day-to-day work exciting, challenging, and rewarding. "I have always felt that it is tremendously satisfying to make a difference—large or small— whether by changing the life of an individual person or by changing a law that affects the nation as a whole," Carol said. Since arriving at the EPA, Carol has made a difference—charting a new course for the agency by promoting a firm commitment to environmental goals along with common sense, innovation, and flexibility in reaching those goals. She is pleased with the aggressive actions of the Clinton administration to pass laws and set standards for air and water quality and for food safety, and to accelerate the cleanup of abandoned and contaminated land. She is also proud of the expansion of the Community Right-to-Know program under what she feels is one of our nation's most important environmental laws. This law has enabled Carol to provide communities with unprecedented access to information about chemicals released into their water and air. "There is no doubt in my mind that an informed and involved local community will always do a better job of protecting the local environment than some distant bureaucracy," she explained.

Carol, a native Floridian, grew up with a great appreciation for the environment and Florida's natural resources. Now that she is married and has a son, she says that she is even more inspired to protect the environment for her son and future generations. "I worry that if my son, Zachary, returns to Miami, the quality of life that I experienced will not be present," she said.

When asked what advice she has for law students or recent graduates, Carol is quick to advocate public service as a part of every lawyer's career path. "In the public sector, recent graduates get greater responsibility and a breadth of experience that the private sector doesn't offer," she says. "It exposes them to a wider group of people and a more challenging set of issues. Public service is an opportunity to give something back to a larger common good."

STANDING BEHIND HER DECISIONS

Kathy Boller-Koch . . .

"What brings me satisfaction is knowing that I have the power to make decisions that can make children's lives better," explains Kathy Boller-Koch, a Magistrate for Hamilton County Juvenile Court in Ohio. As a Magistrate, she presides over hearings that involve delinquency, dependency, child support, and custody cases. "The challenges that I face," notes Kathy, "are determining which decision is truly the best for children, while balancing parental rights with the best interests of children and an imperfect system."

Family influences, volunteer experience, and lifestyle choices all helped to shape Kathy's interests in law and in children. "As an undergraduate," she recalls, "I was interested in both law and medicine. What moved me toward a career in law was the fact that both my father and grandfather were lawyers. I also wanted a career that I could balance with my family life. When I entered law school, I was only 21 years old. I was interested in criminal law and litigation. Because of my experience as a volunteer at Children's Hospital, I also had an interest in prosecuting child abuse cases."

While a law student at the

University of Cincinnati College of Law, Kathy was a law clerk for a small firm where she conducted research and prepared briefs for litigation cases. Her experience in this position touched on personal injury and domestic relation issues. During law school, she also participated in an extern program at the University of Cincinnati that allowed classroom credit for work in a non-profit setting. This experience was a turning point for Kathy. She says, "One of the big changes in deciding which career path to follow came when I externed for ProKids while in law school. I found a way, as an attorney, that I could advocate for the best interests of children, and I really enjoyed it! "

Immediately following law school, Kathy accepted an in-house counsel position. She spent less than a year in that job before memories of her externship led her to contact ProKids. Recalling both her in-house counsel experience and her ProKids externship, Kathy comments, "After law school, I did corporate work for awhile, and it was fun, but it did not give me the same sense of fulfillment. I called ProKids and offered to do pro bono work and instead they offered me a job!"

Kathy's first position at ProKids was as a Contract Attorney carrying a caseload of 70 to 80 cases. She was in court on a daily basis representing juveniles. As an advocate at ProKids, she often worked many more hours than the position description required. Serving the best interests of her "children" necessitated that she respond to the call for help whenever it came.

Kathy also found ways to impact the system. While working closely with the local school district, for example, she discovered that the truancy problem was often overwhelming. She was able to pilot a truancy program on the grade school level that mirrored the one already in existence in the middle school. She felt strongly that early intervention with parents was critical—and that intervention must include education about how the truancy program worked and why it was important for parents to take responsibility for their children's actions. At Vine Elementary School, she worked with parents of preschool children in an informal setting, educating them and encouraging them to get involved and stay involved with their children's education. The school now has an attendance rate greater than 90%. "It's all part of the ability to see a broader picture," Kathy says. "This larger vision helps you to be proactive in your position, not just reactive."

In her current role as a Juvenile Court Magistrate, Kathy has found an even more satisfying way to impact children's lives. Her psychology classes as an undergraduate, her work at ProKids, and her volunteer experience at Children's Hospital all combined to prepare her for her present position. One thing she has found exceptionally challenging has been the changing definition of "family." "I have had to overcome the idea that either I or other professionals know what the perfect family is for a child," Kathy comments. "I have to look independently and with a fresh vision at each new case and child to make the decision that is best for that child. I work with each case carefully so that I am not basing my decision on someone's idea of a 'Brady Bunch' family."

The qualities that Kathy Boller-Koch admires most in her peers—honesty, integrity, hard work, and loyalty—are the same qualities that have led to her own success as a children's advocate. "You have to be comfortable with what you are doing," she comments. "This means that I must stand behind my decisions." She is committed to positively impacting the lives of the children who come to her courtroom. "People come expecting justice," she says. "I expect to be treated with respect, but I also expect to give understanding and respect in return. I feel that it is my obligation to explain why I rule against someone in my court and to educate them about their responsibility. People have actually thanked me after leaving court."

As a Magistrate, Kathy has had to develop listening skills that go beyond the spoken word. Her role demands that she ask probing questions and not accept things at face value. Kathy notes, "It is also my responsibility to make sure that I educate the parents and children that I work with so that they have a better understanding of the law and how it will impact their lives." In addition, Kathy is committed to working to maximize the potential of the "system" to make the lives of children and their families better through education and support.

Reflecting on her career, Kathy says, "I feel that originally the legal field was a noble profession and noble things can still be accomplished. For me, trying to repair families and protect children and hopefully give them a better future is noble. It's something I feel good about. There are tough decisions that I agonize over, but, all in all, I feel good about what I do. I know I could make more money in other areas of law, but I don't think I would be as satisfied."

Follow Your Dream

Phil Fornaci . . .

Current Job:

When interviewed for this book, Phil Fornaci was Legal Services Director for the Whitman-Walker Clinic in Washington, D.C. In July 1996, be became Director of NAPIL Fellowships for Equal Justice, also in Washington.

Career Highlights:

Talk about following your dream. AIDS advocacy was Phil Fornaci's only interest when he considered attending law school. Phil started working for the Whitman-Walker Clinic the day after his last law school exam, and he became head of the legal department there. Now a new position promises new opportunities for Phil to use his law degree to make a real difference to persons in need of legal services.

"This Practice, Sadly, Is Busier Than Ever" proclaimed a headline on the front page of *The Legal Times* on May 20, 1996. The headline was accompanied by a photograph of Phil Fornaci, Legal Services Director of the Whitman-Walker Clinic in Washington, D.C., who was marking his fifth anniversary at Whitman-Walker on May 20—also the day he was interviewed for this book. *The Legal Times* article provided evidence that Phil had achieved one of his goals as Legal Services Director… acquiring more name recognition for the Whitman-Walker Clinic and publicizing how they serve men and women living with AIDS and HIV in the Washington, D.C., metropolitan area. His other goal for Whitman-Walker had been to make their legal program a solid, stable legal resource for people living with AIDS.

One of the first steps Phil took as Legal Services Director was to hire a litigator for Whitman-Walker. Phil says, "I wanted to put the fear of the Lord into evil doers," though he laughingly notes that he is an atheist. But Phil's point is clear: he wanted Whitman-Walker to become more high-profile and to let everyone, especially potential clients, know what it is they do. Whitman-Walker has the largest pro bono program in Washington, D.C., with the largest number of volunteer lawyers (400). Nationally, there are very few programs like the Whitman-Walker Clinic. Phil has definitely let the public know.

Phil Fornaci went to law school knowing what he wanted to do . . . AIDS advocacy. Deciding to attend law school, however, was different from anything else he had done up until that time. Upon graduating from Columbia University, Phil's goal had been essentially to work as little as possible—and to do what he was interested in, which primarily involved activist politics. He worked as a writer and acquired most of his work on a free-lance basis.

While working as a free-lance writer, Phil volunteered at Whitman-Walker as a "Buddy." "It was infuriating to see friends and acquaintances struggling to survive a terrible disease but also struggling for their basic legal rights to work and to get medical care," Phil comments. He felt as if he could make an impact dealing with AIDS issues if he had a law degree. Phil knew he wanted to stay in Washington, D.C., where he was already part of the community and contributing locally. He was accepted at The George Washington University Law School, where, Phil says, "GW was very supportive and paid most of my tuition. They believed me—a 30-year-old entering student—when I said I wanted to do public interest work and was very specific about my goals."

Phil never expected to get a job at Whitman-Walker. He interned at Whitman-Walker in 1989 during law school, knew the legal director well, and always stayed in touch, but there were only two lawyers in Whitman-Walker's legal department at the time. However, in March 1991, Ruth Eisenberg, the legal director, accepted a new job, and Phil started as a staff attorney in May 1991, the day after completing his last law school exam. Phil's biggest selling point when applying for the position at Whitman-Walker was the fact that he was a known commodity. He also knew a great deal about AIDS and about working with people with AIDS.

When Phil started working full-time as a staff attorney at Whitman-Walker, the Clinic's legal department had a three-person staff: the director, Phil, and an administrative assistant. Phil worked with legal director Dinah Wiley for 3 1/2 years, until in 1995 he became legal director himself. In Phil's five years at Whitman-Walker, the program expanded to serve two to three times more people, and the client load increased by 15 to 20% each year.

What kept Phil at Whitman-Walker for five years? "The clients are really great people to work with," he comments, "and it has been a very positive experience. I am actually able to help them." Prior to law school, Phil experienced his own personal grief associated with AIDS and working at Whitman-Walker was a way to channel his energy. "I was a gay man helping gay men in the community, as well as straight people living with AIDS and facing the same issues, making a real difference," Phil says. His motivating force was his desire to create something that wouldn't go away. He wanted to provide the most systematic and comprehensive legal assistance possible. He has achieved that goal too . . . stability in the legal program.

Being Legal Services Director for Whitman-Walker required Phil to wear multiple hats. "It is hard to be a director," Phil says. "It is hard to be a part of a legal program among many medical and social service programs. You have to barter within the organization for different issues, and political issues arise . . . it is a bit much. It is exhausting and way more than one person can do." Phil dealt with staffing, volunteer recruitment and mentoring, fundraising, extra-curricular activities such as writing an "AIDS Advocacy" manual, and the usual director duties including budgets, supplies, space, and policy issues. Phil learned the various duties over his years at Whitman-Walker and says he "grew up with the program." He worked his way up through the ranks and received support from his co-workers when he came up for director. "They wanted me to get the job," Phil says. "My co-workers knew I would be fair, and they knew where I was coming from."

When asked about the difficulties involved with working at Whitman-Walker Clinic, Phil listed several concerns—limited resources, short staffing, and long hours. "There are too many clients, not enough resources," he said. Another challenge stemmed from the fact that Phil's role became more managerial. "Law school doesn't teach you how to manage," Phil commented. "Law school doesn't teach students how to think creatively about how to tackle resource problems. We've got an expanding base of clients," said Phil—"how are we going to serve them and how are we going to get the people and resources to help us do it?" These are practical skills Phil thinks are not being taught in school. He commented, "The thing that helped me the most was my writing ability. Writing is the single biggest marketable skill."

Phil serves as a role model to others, but he had few people to emulate when he started law school. "At that time, the legal aid world was much more heterosexist," Phil comments. "It had its own 'oldboy network.'" At

Whitman-Walker, however, Phil discovered that "there are really promi-nent gay male and lesbian lawyers doing AIDS work that I can associate with, and I can be out at my job and not worry about it. Whitman-Walker is a community organization that I can work for."

When asked about his aspirations, Phil notes that, in addition to realiz-ing he'll never play in the NBA, he has also concluded he will never be a litigator. What really interests Phil is helping people obtain legal services. He has a broader outlook than most lawyers and hopes to continue to broaden his horizons. Shortly before being interviewed for this book, Phil applied for the position of Director of the National Association for Public Interest Law (NAPIL) Fellowships for Equal Justice. NAPIL fellowships fund public service legal work throughout the country, and the position offered Phil an opportunity to work in a public interest organization where he could expand the program and make a real difference. Phil was later offered the position; he accepted and began work in July 1996.

Ironically, one of Phil's biggest obstacles has been the fact that, as he admits, "I am not a generally outgoing person. The Whitman-Walker and NAPIL jobs force me to work with people and network." Phil knows he needs help from a huge number of people, and he knows networking is essential, but, he says, "It's not in my nature." His friends say that he would never make a good waiter. Fortunately, Phil is not a waiter; he's a passionate individual who applies his time and talents to the public interest—definitely someone to emulate.

FINDING A NICHE AS A MEDIATOR

Michael Klingler . . .

CURRENT JOB:

Mediator/Arbitrator, Judicial Arbitration and Mediation Service/Endispute (San Jose, California)

CAREER HIGHLIGHTS:

Career transitions have been a way of life for Michael Klingler. He has been a corporate accountant; a personal injury and business litigator; a staff counsel, transactional lawyer, and general counsel for a bank; a corporate chief financial officer; and a commercial real estate broker. Yet, varied as Michael's past positions have been, they have all combined to provide the perfect background for his current role as a mediator and arbitrator.

Michael Klingler has reinvented himself professionally several times, but his current role as a mediator/neutral capitalizes on all of his multi-faceted background. It is as if all of his previous work experience had been preparing him for this specific position.

When Michael was in college in the '60s, he was required to take ROTC. This resulted in being ordered to go to Vietnam upon graduating with a business degree. But he delayed that obligation for a year while he worked as an accountant at Monsanto and traveled to audit agricultural outlets. He then fulfilled his two-year military commitment with one year in Vietnam and another at a base in the U.S. Upon discharge, he chose to go to law school because, when he was at Monsanto, he had to get approval from the lawyers for much of his work, and he decided he wanted to have that legal knowledge himself. He attended Hastings College of the Law, graduating in 1973. While at Hastings, he met a well-known practicing attorney who told Michael that the only true lawyers were litigators—and who influenced him to become a litigator rather than pursue a master's degree in tax as Michael had intended.

He next obtained a position at a large Oakland firm as a personal injury and business litigator, but he found the litigation process to be too adversarial and perceived it to be wasteful. He decided that he preferred being part of a team and that he wanted an in-house position where he would facilitate business and real estate transactions, do deals, be an advisor, and have one client. To achieve this goal, he actively networked and was invited to join a bank as staff counsel. While with the bank, he was able to transfer to a transactional job by emphasizing his previous experience and his exposure to transactional issues as a litigator. He was promoted to general counsel three years later. Michael found that his in-house position provided him with exposure to many nonlegal issues, because many of the problems that were brought to him were really business issues with a legal subtext. When the bank merged in 1982 with a larger bank that already had its own general counsel, there was no position for Michael. He was asked, however, to stay through the merger to facilitate the transition, and he did so.

Shortly after he left the bank, he met a venture capitalist with a company that was "in trouble." Michael emphasized his financial background to create a position for himself as chief financial officer. He then worked on financial, legal, and deal-making issues 15 hours a day, seven days a week for the next year, until the company was out of trouble. At this point, deciding that it was time to move on and take a long vacation, Michael sold his home and got rid of all of his belongings. For the next eight months, he traveled around the world.

When Michael returned from his travels, he needed to earn an income. So he went through his Rolodex to obtain networking names in order to create fruitful connections for job information. He found the name of a commercial real estate broker who had consulted for the bank where Michael had been general counsel. An information interview with this man piqued Michael's interest, and he decided to work as a commercial real estate broker.

Michael recalled that when he had worked as a lawyer he had disliked real estate brokers. But, as a broker, he became sensitive to the other side of the coin, realizing that lawyers sometimes help kill deals and saddle brokers with heavy responsibilities. This new insight helped Michael transition from law because, as a broker/matchmaker, he learned patience and ways to put together deals without being in a power position. This, in turn, was good training for mediation where the mediator basically brokers the deals—although, unlike real estate brokers, mediators get paid even when deals fail. In retrospect, Michael also feels that it was a good decision to become a litigator because litigation allowed him to see the inside of a law suit and its deficiencies . . . helpful knowledge for both a corporate counsel and a mediator.

After about five years in real estate, Michael started to get bored. Because the real estate market was declining at that time, he began to think about his next step. Even so, he stayed in real estate for two more years because, he says, "I wasn't too unhappy, and I didn't have a good alternative." Then, in 1992, he took a mediation training course and loved it. For him it was a "wow" experience. Mediation put together all of the knowledge and useful negotiation and dispute settlement techniques he had previously learned. He was ready to move into mediation immediately but found no opportunities at that time.

Then, in 1993, the people with whom he had trained needed help in their mediation practice and hired Michael. He loved handling mediations, which he conducted in the construction, probate, employment, homeowner association, general business, personal injury, and real estate areas. After 2 1/2 years, Michael affiliated with the Judicial Arbitration and Mediation Service/Endispute, a national organization of retired judges and lawyers, where he continues to mediate, as well as spend about 20% of his time doing arbitrations. As an arbitrator, he remains involved in the intricacies of the law.

Michael admits that it is still somewhat difficult to be a full-time mediator. Although he believes the climate for mediation is improving, the current market is small and very competitive. In addition, Michael believes the lay and legal communities need further education regarding the process and their expected conduct during a mediation.

Although he used to think that he "hated the litigation system," Michael now realizes that what he needed to find was his own niche—a place where he was comfortable within "the system." Working in mediation, side by side with the traditional litigation system, is that niche for him.

Michael feels very strongly that it is important for anyone whose work is making them miserable to take action—it worked for him. "Instead of waiting until you are so miserable, act on the early signs of distress to avoid the depths," he advises. "You can't give in to the fear which will keep you stagnated. Develop a low tolerance for misery and frustration, and that will help move you along." His further advice—

• "Work hard to position yourself. Redo and tailor your résumé for your targeted position, then spend a lot of time looking."

- "When you're unhappy at work, there's a depressive quality, and it's hard to put out more energy; there's an inertia that must be overcome."

- "A tool to figure out what to do is to write out your ideal work situation as well as the negatives—the people, money, hours, workstyle, etc."

- "Find a life interest thread and follow it; then just take action and do it. Take a small step in any direction, and that will start your forward movement."

. . . Just as Michael did.

TAPPING SKILLS DEVELOPED AS A PARK RANGER

William S. Benish . . .

CURRENT JOB:

West Academic Account Manager for West Publishing Corp., A Division of the Thomson Corporation (New York City)

CAREER HIGHLIGHTS:

Bill Benish worked as a Park Ranger when he was in college and discovered he enjoyed being an instructor and working with people. Following law school, Bill initially pursued a traditional career path as a summer associate and litigation associate before deciding to use the instructional talents he had developed as a Park Ranger to reach out and assist others pursuing a legal education.

As a child, Bill Benish never considered being a lawyer. He was not one of those people who know either from birth or from a family member's career influence that they want to go to law school. In fact, early on, Bill seemed to be leaning toward biology as a major, with medical school a much more likely goal than law school. Born in 1966, he grew up in Bayside, Queens (New York), with an early love of all things in nature. A bright, energetic child, he quickly established himself as a neighborhood authority on the plant life of the area.

Bill enrolled in Manhattan College and chose environmental biology as his major. It was during college that Bill obtained employment as an Urban Park Ranger with the New York City Department of Parks and Recreation. He was assigned to duty in Central Park, a role that was well-suited to his interests in nature and his enjoyment of instructing people on the natural aspects of their habitat. In addition to patrolling and inspecting different areas of the park, Bill's primary responsibility was giving interpretive tours of the park's flora, fauna, historic heritage, and design to visiting school groups, tourists, and dignitaries. Sometimes Bill was responsible for providing a tour with an historic focus for a specially designated group of visitors; other times he answered the questions of inquisitive toddlers out for walks with their parents. Throughout these experiences of dealing with all types of people, Bill demonstrated a patient and kind approach that endeared him to his colleagues as well as to his guests. The atmosphere surrounding the Park Ranger position left Bill with definite ideas on how one should relate to one's "constituents" in a work setting.

During college, Bill decided to opt for law rather than medicine, and he enrolled at New York University Law School. There he followed the long-standing tradition of coursework and summer associate legal employment. Bill admits that during this time he did not feel as though all of his talents were being utilized to their maximum potential.

Immediately following his graduation from law school in 1991, Bill joined a New York law firm as a litigation associate—an experience that was frustrating at best. Bill found little personal satisfaction either in his position or in the type of work he was being given. He wondered whether his temperament was right for the law—and specifically for litigation. He found the attitudes of some of the personnel at the firm frustrating. Yet, sure that law was for him and that being a "people person" and using one's law degree were not mutually exclusive, Bill began speaking with friends and colleagues about their feelings of career satisfaction.

He happened to talk with a friend who was employed by West Publishing Corporation and was delighted with what he learned about this company. Bill interviewed with West in the early fall of 1992 and started working for West immediately thereafter.

Bill has risen in the company and is now a West Academic Account Manager. As such, he combines a field and office position, providing hands-on teaching instruction and coordinating the WESTLAW® Training Programs at four major law schools—Columbia, City University of New York, Rutgers-Newark, and Seton Hall University School of Law. Bill is responsible for training on-line for all first-year law students at these schools. He is also responsible for providing ongoing WESTLAW training and instruction for new faculty members. In addition, Bill designs and formats new programming to assist law students in their first summer associate experience and with their transition from law student to practicing attorney. He feels that these programs are vital because they help build the tangible skills and the confidence of young law students and attorneys.

Bill is tremendously satisfied with his position. As a field position, it combines a great deal of autonomy with the security and stability of working for a major corporation. Bill is constantly in contact with the legal community and able to keep on the cutting edge of the evolving world of on-line legal technology. Yet, it is no surprise that the same factors that provided Bill with tremendous satisfaction in his job as a Park Ranger continue to surface in his present career. Bill truly enjoys teaching. All who come into contact with him remark on his collegial spirit, his broad-based knowledge, and his endless patience. He now has tremendous need for his "people skills" as he instructs students and faculty—both in groups and one on one. Bill is particularly skilled at bringing people of all levels and abilities together and instilling in them the confidence to go forward. He enjoys his interaction with faculty, staff, and students at all four law schools as well as with his colleagues at West. The vast amount of knowledge necessary to keep up with changes in online services poses no problem for Bill. He truly feels he has found the best of all possible worlds using both his law degree and his gift for bringing knowledge to people through any medium.

DOING PUBLIC GOOD——FROM INVESTIGATIONS TO TRIALS

Scott D. Levine . . .

CURRENT JOB:

Deputy Chief, General Crimes
Section, U.S. Attorney's
Office, Northern District of
Illinois (Chicago)

CAREER HIGHLIGHTS:

One measure of Scott Levine's
success is the fact that in
November 1996 he received a
Department of Justice Director's
Award for Outstanding Service
as an Assistant United States
Attorney. He knew he had found
his niche in the law when he
worked as an intern for the U.S.
Attorney's Office during his
third year of law school. Now
his job involves the full spectrum of trial practice—from
investigations to trials to briefs
to oral arguments.

As a federal prosecutor for the U.S. Attorney's Office for the last seven years, Scott Levine has never lost a trial. He has prosecuted fraud, drug, violent crime, tax, embezzlement, public corruption, and organized crime cases and feels particularly strongly about public corruption cases.

Scott knew he had found his niche in the law when he worked as an intern for the U.S. Attorney's Office during his third year at Northwestern University School of Law. During his internship, he got involved in the biggest drug trial in the Northern District of Illinois, and he was hooked. Since the U.S. Attorney's Office was unable to hire Scott immediately following his graduation, he returned to his home state of New York to practice law with the firm of Rosenman & Colin. He visited Chicago three times in September and October to interview with the U.S. Attorney's Office and was offered a position with them in November. It took until the following June for a position to actually open and for the security check to be completed. Scott put that time to good use, however, learning valuable litigation skills in his law firm job.

Scott's passion for his current job is evident from even a brief conversation with him. "I never imagined when I was in law school that I would enjoy the practice of law so much," he comments. "I just love coming to work every day."

Scott was named a Deputy Chief in the General Crimes Section in February 1996. He enjoys that role and wants to continue to grow with the job. He likes trying cases with other assistants, editing briefs, and guiding others by sharing his investigation experiences with them. He also likes being in court.

Few attorneys get to experience the full spectrum of trial practice that Scott enjoys. One of the aspects of his job he likes the most is that he is involved in each case from beginning to end: he participates in the investigations (often jointly with the Federal Bureau of Investigation or the Drug Enforcement Administration), then presents the indictments to the Grand Jury, and then conducts the jury trials. If a case is appealed, he writes the appellate brief to the Seventh Circuit Court of Appeals and makes the oral argument.

The traits he admires most in other trial lawyers are dedication and preparation. These traits are clearly exemplified by Scott's own career, as his comments demonstrate: "I prepare very, very hard. I spend a tremendous amount of time at work, and I prepare my cases so when I get into the courtroom I feel that I have done everything I can to avoid surprise." Scott also admires trial lawyers who have a sense of fairness and justice and of doing the right thing. He feels that he has had very strong mentors in the U.S. Attorney's Office—mentors who have a finely honed sense of justice. He likes being a prosecutor because he is in a position to do public good.

While in law school, Scott enjoyed sitting around the Abbott Hall dormitory exchanging stories with his classmates. He says, "Making an opening statement is a lot like sharing stories in Abbott Hall. A prosecutor's credibility is everything. I'm successful because I'm believable. I'm myself."

The case in which Scott takes the most pride is the one which earned him a Department of Justice Director's Award, which was presented to Scott by Attorney General Janet Reno, for outstanding service as an Assistant United States Attorney. He investigated and brought to trial four Chicago police officers who had robbed people, beaten them, and planted drugs on them. The officers, while on duty and in uniform, had held guns to their victims' heads and threatened to kill them. It was

Scott's dedication, drive, and creativity that brought these four officers to justice. The two primary perpetrators are currently each serving 8 1/2 years in prison.

Scott has also prosecuted a $1 million welfare fraud scheme and has conducted a long-term investigation of "ghost-payrolling," which involves paying salaries and health benefits to people who do not work for a public agency. He convicted more than 20 people who had been involved in "ghost-payrolling" at both the city and county levels. These "ghost-payroll" schemes cost taxpayers over $2 million in salaries and health insurance benefits.

Scott has received many awards for his outstanding work. He has won Department of Justice Special Achievement Awards in 1991, 1994, and 1996, and the International Narcotic Enforcement Officers Association Special Award of Honor in 1992, and a Department of Health and Human Services Special Service Award in 1993.

Outside of work, Scott has taught trial practice at Northwestern University School of Law for the last few years and has also lectured each year at the Department of Justice's annual Public Corruption Conference.

Scott is married and has a 3-year-old son. Although he spends much of his time at work, he makes it a priority to spend time with his family. "The Good Humor truck comes to the neighborhood every Wednesday night," Scott notes, "and unless I'm on trial, I never miss it."

Achieving a Balance in Wyoming

Dona Playton . . .

Dona Playton says she just "fell into law school," but the facts say otherwise. Her interest in law began during high school when she spent three months as an intern in the Wyoming State Legislature. Dona also participated in a high school work study program in which she was assigned to the law firm of Spence, Moriarity and Shuster, P.C.—an experience that further broadened her view of the practice of law and the work of attorneys.

As an undergraduate at the University of Wyoming, Dona majored in administration of justice. After graduating, she pursued what she believed would be the total extent of her legal training: she became a certified paralegal at the University of San Diego's Legal Assistant Program.

Returning to her hometown, Dona discovered that the work of the law in Laramie was accomplished by attorneys with the help of their secretaries, with virtually no use of paralegals. "Law firms in Laramie didn't know how to use a paralegal," Dona says. She had difficulty finding a job and finally settled for contract work for several local firms.

Dona soon realized that her options as a paralegal were limited, yet her interest in practicing law had been piqued. The only logical step was to become an attorney herself. "I sort of ended up in law school," she says. "I didn't put a lot of thought into it. I took the LSAT, was accepted to law school, and there was no turning back."

While attending the University of Wyoming College of Law, Dona was actively involved in clinical programs and gained as much hands-on experience with clients and cases as possible. As the student Director of Legal Services, she oversaw 15 law students who represented indigent clients in several areas of the law. In addition, Dona was President of the Women's Law Forum; she has returned to the law school as an alumna to speak on such issues as sexism in law school and in the profession.

Dona's first position after earning her J.D. was serving as Assistant Attorney General in the area of professional licensing for the State of Wyoming. Dona enjoyed this job, but her 100-mile roundtrip commute took its toll, and after about a year she decided to seek employment closer to home in Laramie.

By staying in touch with contacts in the local legal market, Dona heard that Laramie attorney George Zimmers was retiring, creating an opening in his two-person firm. George Zimmers was to become a very important person in Dona's life. She sent a résumé and followed up with a phone call, which generated an interview. After what she describes as a fruitful conversation, she was very interested in the position. But she heard nothing for several months, even though she knew that no one had been hired.

In a move that distinguishes an active job seeker from a passive one, Dona called Tony Lopez, the firm's remaining partner, and invited him out to lunch. She politely asked him to hire her. He said yes. The deal was done. Why hadn't the firm made a decision sooner? According to Dona, it was simply a case that "sometimes you have to prod them to make a decision." The firm does general practice, including family, real estate, criminal, probate, and personal injury.

Dona enjoys being a lawyer. "I find satisfaction," she says, "in the challenge I face whenever I take on a case and find the resources to advocate in the most efficient, learned, and respectful way I can. Winning for the client means winning for me. That nurtures my competitive nature. When the client and the lawyer can achieve success together, that's a good thing."

Like most lawyers, Dona also has a firm sense of the qualities she admires in other lawyers—particularly the ability to be honest while advocating for clients. "There's a lot of puffery that goes on out there," she comments. "I also appreciate attorneys who can mediate and resolve a matter in a nonadversarial light."

Dona believes she has achieved success in her practice. "Measuring success is very subjective," she notes. "Some do it by the amount of income earned. Some do it by their ability to protect their clients' rights. If I can walk out of the courthouse knowing that I did the best job possible in my representation of my client, then that, to me, is success." Dona also believes that interpersonal skills are a key element in effective and successful lawyering. She sees as her particular strength "my ability to work with people in my field while also advocating for my client and protecting my client's rights."

Although her endeavors in law have been successful, Dona has faced challenges as well. "Balancing my career with my family and social life is a challenge," she comments. She adds, "The bottom line is that women are still the primary caretakers of children." Dona exhorts any prospective lawyers, but especially women, "Before you go to law school, consider very carefully how you will prioritize your life."

Dona has also been challenged to overcome sexism in law school and in practice. "I believe," she states, "that men and women enter law school for different reasons, have different experiences in law school, and experience practice differently as well."

Several anecdotes from her interviewing experiences reveal the sexism she has encountered, particularly in the form of illegal interview questions regarding her marital and family status. In one situation, a male interviewer asked whether she was married. She responded, "Which is better—for me to be married or not?" Undaunted, he immediately followed up with a query into her childbearing plans. In another instance, a male interviewer asked Dona whether her husband would approve of her working. She also interviewed on campus with an employer who selected 15 students to interview—of whom she was the only woman.

But that was all before she came to Zimmers and Lopez. There she not only loves her work but also feels she has the flexibility to achieve a balance that weaves together all of the interesting elements of her life. Because Tony Lopez is a devoted father, he understands how family can sometimes conflict with work. More importantly, however, he also knows that family life enriches people and can complement their on-the-job performance.

One unexpected pleasure Dona has experienced is the unique mentoring relationship she has developed with George Zimmers, the partner who recently retired after 35 years in practice. "He is the type of mentor lawyers dream of," says Dona. "Women don't often receive this type of mentoring. His willingness to spend time with me has boosted my learning, my knowledge, and my confidence. He sees that I am energetic and willing to learn—I don't know it all. He has so much to offer, and I am so willing to learn from it." Dona believes the mentoring relationship is an enriching experience for George as well, affording him the opportunity and the satisfaction of continuing to contribute to the firm that bears his name.

Dona's advice to those preparing for a law career is to gain as much practical experience as possible in trial advocacy, client counseling, and negotiating through law school clinical programs and competitions. "You learn a certain way of thinking in law school. You don't learn how to practice law. Clinical experiences . . . gave me a leg up for practicing law."

Dona's final bit of advice touches on the issue of what makes lawyering satisfying. "Think about who it is you want to advocate on behalf of. Consider whether you want to represent the people or whether you want to represent corporate America. That will make a big difference in your satisfaction."

Born to Be a Judge

Denny Chin. . .

Current Job:

U.S. District Judge, Southern District of New York (New York City)

Career Highlights:

Denny Chin's current position is the culmination of an unusually varied legal career. His private practice experience encompassed large, medium, and small law firms; additionally, his previous government experience included a judicial clerkship and a four-year term as an Assistant U.S. Attorney. He is not only exceptionally well-qualified for his current position but more able than most to make informed comparative analyses of different legal practice settings.

Some experiences in life are so pivotal that one's future path is laid clear. Such was Denny Chin's experience while interning for the Hon. Henry F. Werker, U.S.D.J., S.D.N.Y., during his first summer as a law student at Fordham University School of Law. After coming to law school for rather typical reasons— as an outstanding college student who wasn't sure what to do next— "who" Denny Chin was meant to be and what he was meant to do somehow crystallized in Judge Werker's chambers and courtroom that summer. "From that summer I knew that I would love litigation, I knew that I loved the courtroom; I knew that I wanted to come back to clerk for Judge Werker, and I knew that I wanted to be an Assistant U.S. Attorney," Judge Chin recalls. "I think I probably figured out that I would need to spend a couple of years at a big firm before I got to the U.S. Attorney's Office. I also knew that I would love to come back and be a judge one day."

That Denny Chin went on the accomplish all of this exactly as planned is testimony both to his extraordinary talents and to his determination. The first Asian-American federal district judge to be appointed east of California, Denny Chin is also, at age 42, the second youngest judge in the Southern District of New York. Yet his current position may be seen as the culmination of an unusually varied legal career. After graduation, he returned to Judge Werker's chambers for a two-year clerkship. Denny Chin describes Judge Werker as a jurist who had excellent control of the courtroom and a firm but fair style of treating attorneys—qualities Judge Chin now seeks to display in his courtroom.

After completing the clerkship, he then moved to an associate position at Davis Polk & Wardwell, a large, prestigious, New York City law firm. From this experience Denny Chin says he learned about "quality writing, hard work, and being ethical." He also observed people at the firm who were "terrific litigators, who did not need to shout, who were civil and friendly to their adversaries."

Two years later when the U.S. Attorney's Office, S.D.N.Y., Civil Division, beckoned, Denny Chin answered the call. Trying 12 federal cases in his first two years as an Assistant U.S. Attorney provided an invaluable segue to his current position. Working on behalf of the government, freed from the obligation of generating business and billable hours, then, like now, Denny Chin enjoyed the freedom of being able to "simply do what you think is right and fair."

Four years later, he was ready to move on again and took the somewhat atypical move (for someone with judicial ambitions) of opening a small law firm with two of his Civil Division colleagues from the U.S. Attorney's Office. It was at Campbell, Patrick & Chin that Denny Chin began—quite unintentionally—to develop an expertise in labor and employment law. "I was contacted about a prospective age discrimination case—in fact, I didn't want to take the case," Judge Chin recalls. "But eventually I took it, brought suit, and obtained a very good settlement; the next day I had another half dozen people calling, and it just developed into a labor practice." Eventually 40% of Denny Chin's time at Campbell, Patrick & Chin came to be devoted to labor and employment law. At this time he was also introduced by fellow partner Susan Campbell to Vladeck, Waldman, Elias & Englehard, P.C., a 30-attorney, New York firm focused virtually exclusively on labor and employment law. Vladeck, Waldman began to refer cases to Denny Chin and, upon Campbell, Patrick & Chin's dissolution in 1990, Denny Chin joined this labor firm. After four years as a partner at Vladeck, Waldman, he applied for a judicial position, and he was appointed a U.S. District Judge (S.D.N.Y.) by President Clinton in 1994.

A look at Denny Chin's personal background adds emphasis to his achievements and provides insights into his natural talent for labor law. Born in Hong Kong, Denny Chin emigrated to the U.S. when he was two years old and grew up in Hell's Kitchen, a tough neighborhood in Manhattan. His mother and father, who worked long and hard hours as a seamstress and a Chinese restaurant cook, respectively, instilled in Denny values he has not forgotten. "For me," he says, "being Asian-American has been a strength . . . our culture teaches us to respect our elders and to work hard. My parents certainly insisted that I work hard in school, and education was very important. That was a plus for me. I've worked hard, and I think that's the key." These values help to explain why, had the judicial position not worked out, Denny feels he would still be at Vladeck, Waldman advocating on behalf of individuals who have been discriminated against by their employers. Recollecting the things he liked most about this experience beyond the legal challenges and courtroom time involved, Denny Chin recalls with satisfaction the sense of "doing public interest work in a private sector context."

Now Judge Chin hears not only employment law cases but also criminal law cases, intellectual property law cases, and a variety of cases on miscellaneous matters ranging from children's clothing to the diamond industry. It is the breadth of the substantive areas involved plus the level of responsibility that make this position so challenging, according to Judge Chin. A constant commitment to learning new areas of the law is required, and, with roughly 25 to 30 new cases presented to Judge Chin per month, effective case management is also crucial, as is being an effective mediator. "I try very hard to settle cases," he comments. "In the most difficult ones, you need to defuse, to get some of the emotion out of it— you need to get the parties to be more realistic and practical about it and to help them understand the ramifications of losing." At times simply allowing both parties to air their grievances effectuates settlement, while in other instances encouraging the parties to engage in dialogue leads the case to closure without the necessity of a trial. Overall, however, Judge Chin tries about 20 cases a year.

Judge Chin's experience has solidified his faith in the American judicial system on a number of different levels. First of all, he finds the federal system by which he was appointed a judge "one of the most democratic processes around—remarkably unpolitical." Procedures vary from state to state, but in New York the process works as follows: an application is filed and submitted to the Senator's Screening Committee; the Screening

Committee and, eventually, the Senator interview the finalists; and then the Senator recommends one candidate to the White House for each vacancy. Although Judge Chin recognizes that recommendations and references from his colleagues were important, he found that political connections *per se* did not seem to be a factor. From his current point of view, Judge Chin finds that the Federal Court, at least, moves cases along in an expeditious way and that the jury system works well. "Most of the jury verdicts I've gotten have been right and fair," Judge Chin comments. He adds, "I feel good in the sense that I think justice is being administered in an even-handed way."

A colleague once remarked that Denny Chin was "born to be a judge." If having a calm manner, intelligence, patience, and stamina are helpful predispositions to a judicial career, they have been amply augmented by Denny Chin's more active qualities of vision, hard work, and determination.

FLOURISHING IN THE SPOTLIGHT

Jerri A. Blair . . .

CURRENT JOB:

Partner, Blair & Reid (Tavares, Florida)

CAREER HIGHLIGHTS:

Jerri Blair enjoys the diversity of her private practice, but it is her pro bono cases that have brought her national attention and enabled her to positively influence Florida law. For example, she represented Gregory K., the first minor to initiate a legal action to terminate his parental relationships in order to be adopted by his foster parents. Jerri Blair has also become known for her DNA expertise, a legal area now contributing to a new career twist which may again land Jerri in the spotlight. She has begun writing fiction and is now at work on her first movie script, a murder mystery that will help to spread her message to a wider audience.

Jerri Blair wanted a career where she could make a difference. Blessed with a scientific mind, she earned her undergraduate degree in zoology and hoped ultimately to attend medical school. After attending graduate school in environmental engineering and working as a research assistant for a few years, she concluded that she could have a greater impact on society if she studied law.

Jerri graduated with honors from the University of Florida College of Law. Following her graduation, she moved to Leesburg, Florida, to work for a sole practitioner. Jerri, who was very close to her family, decided to start her own practice in nearby Tavares. Her practice focuses on trial and appellate work with an emphasis on commercial litigation, landlord/tenant disputes, local government law, constitutional law, and children's issues. She enjoys the diversity of her practice and has developed a wonderful list of clients which includes a management company, a municipality, and a number of corporations for which she handles product liability litigation. Her scientific background and objectivity have proven to be an asset in her practice, and she has earned the reputation as Lake County's "premier expert" on DNA. But it is her pro bono cases—mostly on behalf of children—which have provided Jerri with the opportunity to make the greatest impact and have thrust her into the national spotlight.

The case that grabbed the most media attention was the landmark Gregory K case. Jerri represented a 12-year-old boy who was the first minor to initiate a legal action to terminate his parental relationships in order to be adopted by his foster parents. Calling the case a "divorce case," the media descended on Tavares and Jerri. Jerri was invited to be a guest on virtually every talk show. While she declined most—including Phil Donahue—she chose to appear on Larry King Live to share her message. Jerri's message is simple, straightforward, and heartfelt: Children have rights and deserve their day in court.

In another case of national significance, Jerri represented a 15-year-old girl, known only as T.W., who was seeking an abortion without parental consent. Clinic employees informed the girl that, according to state law, she would need a judge's consent, and the girl filed the appropriate paperwork. The judge hearing the case appointed Jerri to represent the girl and another local attorney to represent the fetus. Although neither lawyer had a particular interest in the abortion issue, both found themselves immersed in a case that was drawing national attention. Because the girl was already 10 weeks pregnant, time was crucial. In a matter of days, the case made its way to the U.S. Supreme Court—and the briefs filed by Jerri and by opposing counsel in the case became the first briefs to be filed with the Court via facsimile. The Supreme Court cleared the way for the Florida teen to have an abortion without parental or judicial consent.

Jerri's interest in representing children was cultivated early in her career when she had the opportunity to represent Florida's Department of Health and Rehabilitative Services. She is still brought to tears when reflecting on some of those early cases. "I have seen a huge number of cases that are all so horrible you can't even begin to describe the terror and the horror that children live through," she comments. "No one hears about it because the press is not allowed into hearings that deal with these issues to protect the confidentiality of the children. That's good in some ways, but it's also harmful because it results in the public not being aware of these problems. You can't feel it in your gut until you see what happens to children who are caught in these situations," she says. Jerri has seen a lot and feels compelled to fight to make it easier for children who are caught in the system. "I have been very privileged to represent some very determined minors who have helped to change the status of the law in Florida in very positive ways," she adds.

Due to her expertise in the area of DNA evidence, Jerri has been sought out to handle certain criminal cases and death row appeals. Through these experiences, she has seen that the abuse and neglect suffered by children often leads to criminal behavior. "Our country is in danger of rotting from within," she says, "because the abuse is creating people who will only contribute to society in a harmful way." Jerri feels she can best serve the community by helping children before the "layers of experiences" have had a chance to set in.

Given all that Jerri has observed and experienced, she claims, "I really can't believe I've only been a lawyer for 10 years." And her career path—still in the making—is about to take a new twist. Having seen firsthand how information spreads via the media and entertainment industries, Jerri has begun writing fiction and working on a movie script to further share her message. Relying on her scientific background, the movie will be a murder mystery involving DNA evidence. So . . . Jerri Blair may soon find herself in the spotlight once again.

A Beacon on Behalf of Her People

Tonya Gonnella Frichner . . .

CURRENT JOB:

President, American Indian Law Alliance (New York City)

CAREER HIGHLIGHTS:

Tonya Gonnella Frichner has worked tirelessly and effectively on behalf of her people. She has devoted her efforts to ensuring the constitutional rights, cultural dignity, and environmental security of all Native Americans not only through her position with the American Indian Law Alliance, but also through teaching, writing, and numerous volunteer involvements.

A member of the Onondaga Nation, Snipe Clan of the Haudenosaunee, Tonya Gonnella Frichner was born and raised on her people's territory. She is the oldest of the eight children of Maxine Nolan Gonnella and the late Henry L. Gonnella, Sr., and notes that it was her family, particularly her mother and her mother's people, who instilled in Tonya her firmly rooted values and a strong desire to dedicate herself to serving the needs and interests of Native Americans. "I enjoy what I am doing because I am working for my people," says Tonya, in a simple, candid statement that reflects the commitment to humble service she has built her life upon.

Tonya seems indefatigable as she lives out her commitment to her people. She is the founder and current president of the American Indian Alliance in New York City, and she is an Associate Professor of Native American Law and an author—and, in addition, she devotes her energies to numerous organizations working on behalf of Native Americans. But Tonya's community involvement began long before she started law school. She attended St. John's University in New York City. There she was a Dean's List student, a member of *Who's Who Among Students in American Universities*, and a member of the St. Vincent's College Honor Society.

From 1975 to 1982, prior to attending law school, Tonya served the Native American community through her involvement as Support Services Director and Chair of the Board of Directors of the American Indian Community House, located in New York City. The Community House, through its 15-member board, administers vital health, economic, and occupational services programs for more than 14,000 Native American constituents throughout the New York City area. During her involvement with the Community House, Tonya conducted extensive research to analyze the pressing needs and concerns of the Native American community. Demonstrating innovative leadership, she helped establish and supervise occupational training programs and an array of services designed to assist with the diverse cultural, social, and employment needs of the Native American population in the area.

Another significant role that Tonya was called upon to play was that of fundraiser. In this capacity she had to approach potential sources of funding through a variety of means, including grant applications and appeals to private and public entities. In an era of decreased funding to not-for-profit, minority organizations, she continually met with success. A consistent goal for Tonya was to maintain and increase public awareness of the Native American community—and of the needs of Community House and its constituents. To this end, Tonya designed a lecture series to provide the public with knowledge of Native American issues.

In 1982, Tonya founded and served as director for CORN (Circle of Red Nations). Funded entirely by the private sector, CORN devoted its efforts to serving Native American people from North, South, and Central America on a 24-hour basis. The center assisted with basic living needs as well as seeking to provide occupational training and events designed to strengthen community awareness. Once again, as director, Tonya was not only responsible for administration, budget, fundraising, and grant applications but also served as a liaison to government agencies and the private sector. Tonya herself staffed the center late into the evening when a crisis was at hand.

Through her community leadership roles, Tonya became convinced of the crucial need for adequate legal representation for Native Americans in areas ranging from constitutional and civil rights issues to environmental impact litigation. Tonya enrolled in the J.D. program of the City

University of New York Law School at Queens College, a program devoted to training public interest lawyers. While gaining invaluable knowledge from her legal studies, Tonya distinguished herself in many ways. Her fellowship honors included the Sequoyah Fellowship, Association on American Indian Affairs; the Special Scholarship in Law for American Indians; the American Indian Fellowship, U.S. Department of Education; the Law Students Civil Rights Research Council Fellowship; and the American Indian Scholarships Fellowship. During law school, Tonya created a new brainchild—the First Annual American Indian Law Symposium at Columbia University Law School, for which she acted as Symposium Director. This event drew more than 500 grassroots delegates and legal scholars from around the world.

Tonya enhanced her legal experience through her summer jobs during law school. She was a law clerk for the firm of Steven, Hinds and White, P.C., in New York City, where she researched and wrote on issues involving constitutional and international law. She also served as a summer associate for the New York State Department of Law's Litigation Bureau, researching class action suits against the state of New York. While there, she designed a seminar for the Attorney General's staff and summer program on the topic of legal analysis of constitutional issues.

After earning her Juris Doctor degree in 1987, Tonya remained fervently committed to serving the needs of Native American peoples throughout the world. In 1987, she served as a delegate to and legal counsel for the Haudenosaunee people at the Fifth Session of the United Nations Subcommission on Human Rights/Working Group on Indigenous Populations held in Geneva, Switzerland. During the following nine years, she returned for subsequent sessions and also served on the Preparatory Committee for the United Nations Conference on Environment and Development in New York City.

As President of the American Indian Law Alliance in New York City, Tonya is using her legal expertise on behalf of her people. The Alliance is a not-for-profit organization that "focuses primarily on legal issues affecting all aspects of Indian survival and whose mandate is quite simply to serve the people." And serve it has done and continues to do on a wide range of concerns. Through the Alliance, Tonya played a significant role in assuring the participation of Indigenous Peoples and Native Nations at the 1992 International Environmental Earth Summit in Rio de Janeiro, Brazil. The Alliance provides direct legal assistance free of charge to New York's Native American population through intake, representation, and referral.

In addition to her role with the American Indian Law Alliance, Tonya is an Associate Adjunct Professor of Native American Law at the Greenberg Center for Legal Education and Urban Policy at the City College of New York and is a visiting professor at Hunter College and New York University. Tonya's far-reaching service to others includes being legal counsel and program director for the Iroquois National Lacrosse Team, the official team of the Haudenosaunee tribes. She accompanied the team to the International Lacrosse Federation's world games in Perth, Australia, when the team competed for the first time as an independent nation.

Tonya's voice continues to be heard through the many organizations to which she devotes her indefatigable efforts. She is on the Board of Visitors of the Greenberg Center for Legal Education and Urban Policy at the City College of New York; a cofounder of the Roundtable of Communities of Color; a member of the Advisory Board of the City University of New York Dispute Resolution Consortium; and a member of the Board of Directors of IMADR—the International Movement Against All Forms of Discrimination and Racism. Tonya also cofounded the Native American Council of New York City and, through this group, brought her people into an alliance to speak on the 500th anniversary of the arrival of Christopher Columbus in the Western Hemisphere. In 1993, she was named American Indian of the Year by the Thunderbird American Indian Dancers—a group Tonya cherishes both for the beauty of their performances and for their portrayal and preservation of Native American culture.

There seems to be no end to Tonya's energy. As long as her people experience injustice and as long as there is a need to make others aware of the issues facing Native American peoples at home and abroad, Tonya will continue to offer a new idea or a fresh way to heighten understanding and compassion amongst all peoples of the earth. Amid her many involvements, she somehow also manages to find free time to enjoy with her husband, businessman and professor Herb Frichner.

In 1996, Tonya Gonnella Frichner was the recipient of the Helen Hunt Neighborhood Leadership Award bestowed by the New York Women's Foundation. In 1990, Tonya was honored with the Ellis Island Medal of Honor in recognition of her work on behalf of her people. How appropriate that this medal, conceived in the shadow of the Statue of Liberty, should go to this woman, who stands as a beacon for her people and for all that "liberty and justice for all" implies.

CARPE DIEM...CARPE DIEM...
CARPE DIEM...CARPE DIEM...

Sean A. Joell Johnson. . . .

CURRENT JOB:

Counsel for Law and Business Affairs, MTV—Music Television (New York City)

CAREER HIGHLIGHTS:

Sean's motto—*carpe diem*—flashes across his computer as his screen saver. In his career, Sean has certainly seized the opportunities that have come his way. Networking, persistence, and hard work were the keys to achieving his present position at MTV. During his law school summers, he worked for the Paramount Pictures Motion Picture Group and Motown Records. Upon graduation from law school, Sean obtained a position with Black Entertainment Television, which in turn led to his present job at MTV.

Sean Johnson looks out at the Hudson River from his office window at MTV, where he is Counsel for Law and Business Affairs. He is involved in all aspects of negotiating and drafting agreements related to MTV programming—series, specials, news, sports, music—including talent, production-related, and programming acquisition agreements, licensing and intellectual property, general corporate transactional matters, and day-to-day legal production issues. He is happy as an MTV attorney. "It's a lot of work and a lot of responsibility," Sean says. "MTV maintains a growing, fast, hectic pace. It is not structured like a normal corporation."

When Sean travels, he takes his laptop, cell phone, and modem for e-mail. He is well-equipped and never out of reach. The best part, he admits, is that casual dress is the standard at MTV. At the time he was interviewed for this book, he was wearing jeans and a sweater, which he says is everyday wear. "MTV is a nice place, and the attorneys are exceptional," Sean comments.

In addition to Sean, MTV's legal department includes four other attorneys, four paralegals, and a number of assistants. Each attorney specializes in an area. Sean handles shows out of development and deals with venue and production. He also works on a great number of copyright issues.

How does an attorney arrive at MTV? Sean worked for Black Entertainment Television (BET) at a time when they were working with MTV on the Urban Aid Project—a major R&B benefit concert. Originally, BET and MTV were to coproduce the concert. As other issues developed, BET's role changed from coproducing the concert to licensing it. Sean dealt with the matter effectively and professionally, and several months later he received a call requesting that he come interview at MTV for an open position.

What Sean likes best about lawyering is solving the puzzle, putting the pieces together, especially when working with producers. He also enjoys working collectively on creative teams to provide legal advice. "I see the big picture," says Sean. That is one of his many contributions to a creative team. Sean also maintains an incredible amount of autonomy. He handles the basic legal portion of his job on his own and brings in various parties—creative or business—on given issues. While enjoying this autonomy, Sean notes that everyone at MTV works together. "You can't be an island here. You won't survive." There is a great balance of autonomy and team work at MTV.

How has Sean achieved his success?

When Sean decided to enroll in The George Washington University Law School, he didn't know where he would eventually work. After graduating from the University of Southern California, he spent one year as a business manager at a performing arts theater. He enjoyed his job, but he wanted to do more and to make more money. Upon consulting his mentor for advice, Sean decided to become a lawyer. He knew going into law school that he would one day work in entertainment. He did not, however, envision ever living in New York City or working at MTV. He had always hated NYC and says his friends still find it hard to believe that he is in NYC or even on the East Coast; he hails from California. Sean realizes he has to be in a major city to work in entertainment law, and, if he has to be in NYC for a while, he has decided that's okay.

Networking has been the key to Sean's success. He enjoys meeting people, and he is good at it. Even more impressive, he likes to listen to people. "Everybody has something to say, whether you agree with what they are saying or not," he comments. "People love to talk about themselves and give advice." To illustrate, Sean tells a story about going to lunch with one of his mentors, a film producer in Los Angeles who spent the entire lunch talking about himself. Sean just kept nodding his head and saying, "Yes, I see, uh-huh." The producer walked away thinking, "That was a great lunch." Sean laughs at the end of this story but adds that luck is where opportunity meets preparation. He means it.

An important part of networking for Sean is persistence. When trying to obtain a summer job at Motown Records during law school, he sent his résumé and then called about every two weeks from approximately February to April until he got an interview. He developed a rapport with the assistant answering the phone, and she encouraged the contact person to give Sean a chance. He was different from the other callers—he sounded like a very nice guy, she said. For this job as for every other job Sean obtained, he first laid the ground work. When he was working at BET, he sent Christmas cards to the people at MTV he had worked with on the benefit concert. He received a call the next month to interview. "Always keep in contact," Sean says.

Networking and persistence do not pay off without hard work, however. Sean established a foundation for his professional network while working at Paramount Pictures Corporation during the summer after his first year of law school. But he had to work hard. "It makes you humble," he said, "and I was happy to have the opportunity." At Paramount, someone told Sean that the best thing he could do was to make himself indispensable—to be "the one they call." With hard work, says Sean, this can happen in any work setting. "Even when you network," he notes, "you still have to prove yourself."

As far as law school grades, Sean never thought they predicted how well he would perform as an attorney. He believes in the practical over the theoretical and adds, "I know lots of people doing very well with middle-of-the-road grades." Two of Sean's extracurricular activities were being SBA President and Director of the Small Business Clinic while at GW Law School. These activities helped him learn how to deal with people, and, he says, "They were a source of great personal growth." In the Small Business Clinic, he dealt with clients and the legal aspects of starting a business. As SBA President, he dealt with law students, who, he admits, were "a tough bunch."

None of Sean's fabulous jobs came easily. At the end of his first year of law school he still had no summer job and wasn't sure he'd get the

Paramount job until he finally got the call for an interview. At graduation a number of opportunities fell through. It was not until two months after taking the bar that he received a call from BET. During those two months, Sean traveled and worked at temporary jobs while he waited for a position at BET to open up. He adds, "I wasn't even sure that MTV was going to come through." But it did.

Sean has a number of mentors who have been helpful over the years. "I could name at least five mentors from high school to college to places where I worked," he says. He adds that he "needs the opinions of educated people to help make the right decisions."

Sean has always lived by the motto *carpe diem*—"seize the day"—and it flashes across his computer as his screen saver. His other motto, which he says keeps him grounded, is, "Be ashamed to die until you've achieved some victory for humanity." These two mottoes define Sean Johnson: he's moving forward but keeping his feet on the ground, even at MTV in New York City.

A LEADER AT THE FRONTIERS OF ANALYSIS AND ACTION

Jonathan Wiener . . .

CURRENT JOB:

Associate Professor, Duke University School of Law (Durham, North Carolina)

CAREER HIGHLIGHTS:

Jonathan Wiener's "comprehensive approach" to global climate change policy was at the core of the international treaty signed at the Rio Earth Summit in 1992, and he drafted climate change policy for both the Bush and Clinton administrations. A public policy innovator, Jonathan's zeal for the interconnections among the environment, law, society, science, economics, and human health is matched by an equal passion for community building in his own academic and civic community. Jonathan clerked for federal judges Stephen Breyer and Jack Weinstein.

Duke University School of Law Professor Jonathan Wiener is at the forefront of a new generation of policy innovators who are rethinking and reshaping U.S. and global law to meet the challenge of health and environmental risks. At Duke, Jonathan holds a primary appointment at the Law School and a joint appointment at Duke's Nicholas School of the Environment, a combination that underscores and furthers his interest in the interconnections among law, society, science, economics, human health, and the environment.

In the summer of 1992, Jonathan Wiener sat in the heart of the Brazilian Amazon rainforest, thrilling in the knowledge that the new international treaty on climate change—signed at the Rio Earth Summit a day earlier by over 100 countries—incorporated at its core his effort to translate interconnectedness into practical policy. In 1989, international efforts to combat global warming had been stuck in a narrow rut, at loggerheads over a single aspect of the problem—fossil fuel burning. Amidst this impasse

Jonathan Wiener formulated and championed a new "comprehensive approach" to global climate change policy, an innovative idea which fundamentally reshaped the global debate and became the linchpin of the internationally adopted treaty regime. "Perhaps what was most exciting to me as I sat below the Amazon canopy was the prospect that my work to devise and broker the comprehensive approach to global climate policy would directly encourage the conservation of the world's dwindling forests," he notes.

This story of policy innovation reflects precisely the kind of intellectual interconnection that Jonathan came to Duke Law School to pursue. He brings a background in law, economics, and science and hopes to nurture a new union among these perspectives: reintegrating our fractured environmental laws and redefining progress in terms of results. The law is not now, if it ever has been, an autonomous discipline, and the study and practice of environmental and regulatory law demands a multi-disciplinary approach. Jonathan comments, "I was particularly attracted to Duke by the concentration of outstanding strengths it offers in so many critical fields: with world-class experts on environmental and regulatory policy in disciplines such as law, environmental sciences, economics, political science, public policy, and business, Duke has perhaps the strongest faculty of any university in the United States in this area." Jonathan teaches courses in Environmental Law, Global Environmental Law and Property, Mass Torts, and Risk Regulation. He also directs the Cummings Colloquium on Environmental Law, an annual conference series jointly sponsored by the Schools of Law and Environment.

Jonathan arrived at Duke in 1994 after spending seven years learning the practical realities of law in a complex world. After graduating from Harvard Law School in 1987, he clerked for two of the nation's finest jurists, federal trial judge Jack Weinstein in New York and then federal appeals judge (now Supreme Court Justice) Stephen Breyer in Boston. With Judge Weinstein, Jonathan worked on the famous Agent Orange mass tort case, helping to design the distribution of the settlement fund to the large class of Vietnam veterans. In 1989, he moved from the judicial to the executive branch, working first in the Environment Division of the Justice Department, then at the White House Office of Science and Technology Policy, and then at the White House Council of Economic Advisers. In each position he functioned as a policy entrepreneur, developing better ways to address such issues as global climate change, forest conservation, air pollution, risk assessment, and biotechnology. He was a professional senior staff member in both the Bush and Clinton administrations, helping to draft policy on climate change and regulatory review for both Presidents.

Jonathan's zeal for environmental issues was inspired by the early Earth Day celebrations: in the seventh grade he served as his school district's delegate to a state-wide mock environmental legislature, and, despite the fact that all of the other delegates were high school students, young Jonathan was elected chair of a committee and shepherded a land conservation bill to the floor of the full assembly. Later, as captain of the debate team at Harvard, Jonathan became the nation's foremost collegiate advocate on such topics as climate change, pesticides, and hazardous air pollutants.

Jonathan has now broadened and extended his work on comprehensive environmental law toward a thorough redesign of our risk regulation edifice. His recent book, *Risk vs. Risk: Tradeoffs in Protecting Health and the Environment* (Harvard University Press, 1995), examines the ubiquitous phenomenon of risk-risk trade-offs: situations in which efforts to protect against one risk induce new risks.

Jonathan also keeps busy in the public policy arena. His work on risk policy reform has earned him invitations to testify before the U.S. Senate on pending risk legislation, to advise the President's Council on Sustainable Development on risk-based regulatory policy, to draft the report issued by a blue-ribbon panel of legal and economics experts on regulatory reform, and to speak at numerous conferences. In addition, he continues to work on the development of international environmental law; he recently produced a study for the Organization for Economic Cooperation and Development on transactions costs in international markets for environmental protection, and he is now working on a study for the United Nations Conference on Trade and Development.

Interconnectedness is not only an intellectual perspective on complex environmental and economic systems. It is also an ethic of community, and in the short time he has been at Duke, Jonathan Wiener has made a world of difference to the community. He initiated and continues to organize a twice-annual community service day, dubbed "Duke Law School: Dedicated to Durham," in which hundreds of students, faculty, and staff fan out across Durham to work in homeless shelters, soup kitchens, community gardens, and countless other organizations. "Dedicated to Durham" is now an official part of orientation for every incoming student, as well as a spring event for the entire school.

Jonathan's dedication to community work blossomed when he organized a similar event for the fifth reunion of his college class and, in the process, happened to meet a classmate he hadn't really known—now his wife, Ginger Young. Ginger and Jonathan then helped organize the first "servathon" event for the City Year youth service corps in Boston, which today has grown to be the largest such event in the country. Jonathan served as the environmental adviser to the new Americorps–National Service program in 1993, is currently a member of the North Carolina state commission on national and community service, and is also on the board of the Campus Outreach Opportunity League, a national support network for campus-based community service programs.

Jonathan's combination of passion for community building and sober analysis of regulatory policy reflects the imprint of his early mentors. He grew up on environmentalism and economics, ambition and compassion. Today, in response to the challenge to see the complex interconnections of life, Jonathan is a leader in the new frontier of thinkers and doers who are designing smarter law toward better results.

DRINK DEEP OR TASTE NOT THE PIERIAN SPRING

Steven Bryan & Doug Denney . . .

CURRENT JOBS:

Steven Bryan is President and Co-founder of the Pierian Spring Software Company (Portland, Oregon); Doug Denney is Controller of the company.

CAREER HIGHLIGHTS:

Steven Bryan and Doug Denney are law school classmates who now work for the educational software company Steven co-founded. Both pursued joint J.D./Master of Management degrees. Steve launched his company while still in law school and began business with only two employees—himself and his co-founder. Today, Pierian Spring employs 63, one of whom is its Controller, Doug Denney. Doug worked as an Assistant Controller for a manufacturer and then in a law office before being offered a job with Pierian Spring. Steve, on the other hand, always has been— and believes he always will be— an entrepreneur. Steve and Doug both have found perfect ways to combine all of the things in life that are important to them.

Neither Doug Denney nor Steven Bryan has ever gone about his career in a traditional way. Both, for example, attended law school without expecting to practice law, and neither is practicing law today. Both have a strong interest in business and have, in a sense, created their own career paths—Steve through his strong entrepreneurial drive and Doug through his ability to generate job offers even in markets where jobs were scarce.

But the first question that arises about their current careers is not about their individual backgrounds but about their company's name. Why "Pierian Spring"? The name comes from Greek mythology. In ancient Macedonia, nine goddesses were known as the muses of the nine disciplines considered essential for the well-rounded citizen—the arts, science, mathematics, culture, etc. According to mythology, these muses drew their inspiration from a well in the town of Pieria known as the Pierian Spring. Author Alexander Pope referred to this spring in an oft-quoted statement: "A little learning is a dangerous thing. Drink deep or taste not the Pierian Spring."

The name fits the Pierian Spring Software Company, which develops educational software used by schools to support their curriculums in language arts, math, science, and cultural studies. The primary market for the company's CD-ROM-based products is public schools in the United States, but Pierian Spring also receives orders from Canada, Mexico, Southeast Asia, New Zealand, and Great Britain.

Steve Bryan's entrepreneurial tendencies were emerging even before law school. While growing up, he lived all over the United States, graduating from high school in 1976 and then serving in the military. Following that, he worked for the *Wall Street Journal* for nine years in what he describes as a "low-level supervisory position" in Palo Alto. The *Journal* had just developed the satellite communication technology to print its newspaper simultaneously at regional facilities across the country. While working at the *Journal*, Steve attended college at night, almost completing his bachelor's degree. His entrepreneurial side was already emerging, as evidenced by his realization that he "didn't want to work for 20 years just to get to mid-level management" in a corporate environment. "I pictured myself," says Steve, "in a small group of people, doing something fun and interesting and high-tech."

In 1987, he left the *Journal* and entered a program at Willamette that allowed him to finish his B.S. degree quickly and then begin graduate-level study. Although his initial interest was business, the joint J.D./Master of Management degree program offered by Willamette University College of Law seemed to offer the best educational opportunity—and the best support for his goal of starting a company. "I approached law school from a business perspective," Steve comments. "I knew that my entrepreneurial side was coming out . . . I had real life experience. I . . . could read cases in a textbook and immediately match them to experiences I had had."

While still in law school, Steve began the process of getting his company off the ground. He prepared a business plan, found a partner who was "a technical, genius-guru type of guy," explored markets, spoke with professional educators about his potential product, and found investment capital. When asked how he happened to focus on educational software, Steve responds, "Both my grandfather and my father had a great influence on me regarding the importance of the value of education. I had young kids. I had an interest in doing something to help them out in school. I saw a way to bring those things together."

Although he has never practiced law *per se*, Steve feels that his legal training is an invaluable asset. "As CEO," he says, "I probably spend 30% of my time dealing with contracts and licensing agreements and their implications." He adds that complex contract issues are typical of the software industry.

The growth of Pierian Spring has been rapid, and Steve would now like to expand the company by developing new products that address a broader age range. His greatest satisfaction comes, he says, from "producing jobs and products that do good." He derives satisfaction also from seeing his company make a profit, from creating jobs, and from his appreciation of the products themselves. He thrives on hearing success stories about children who were turned on to learning with the help of one of his products.

Only one thing is clear about Steve's future: "I am an entrepreneur now," he says. "I don't think I could ever go back." As for his own success, Steve is modest. "If I've done anything," he comments, "it's to hire the smartest people I can find."

One of those people is Pierian Spring's Controller, law school classmate and fellow "nontraditional law grad" Doug Denney. Like Steve, Doug's career path was nontraditional even before law school. After finishing college with a business degree, he interviewed successfully with a number of companies but decided against the 9 to 5 world. He wanted instead, he says, to "have fun," so he moved to a resort area in Oregon and got a job cutting up potatoes in the kitchen of the Timberline Lodge. He was quickly promoted to the purchasing office. "That wasn't fun enough and didn't pay enough," Doug comments, "so I went into bartending, which was a lot more fun and a lot more money. Then I moved up to managing the winter ski bar." He took two "sabbaticals" for extensive travel forays, then returned to Timberline.

Doug took the LSAT because, he says, "I wanted to be able to tell people I could have gone to law school." After the LSAT he went to Europe, where, he says, he became "infatuated with the idea of going to law school." His bartending experience had made him aware of his strong people skills. "I wanted to add technical skills to my career portfolio," Doug explains, "especially accounting and law. I felt that if I got these technical skills, nothing could stop me. I'd be able to go anywhere, do anything, meet any people. And it worked!"

He chose Willamette University College of Law because of its four-year joint J.D./M.B.A. program. During the summer of his third year, he went to Alaska looking for work. Although he had written to several employers prior to traveling, nothing had come of his letters. He went to Alaska anyway and got a job as a law clerk in five days. He fell in love with Anchorage, but chose not to remain there, preferring to live in Oregon.

Doug returned to Oregon for his last year of law school, graduated, was married, and moved to Bend, Oregon, despite some concerns about its sparse population and lack of professional opportunities. Ten days after arriving in Bend, he had two attractive job offers from manufacturing companies. When asked how he succeeded so quickly, Doug responds: "Part of it is my work ethic. Part of it is my joint degrees. Part of it is my personality." He followed the classic formula for finding a job. He went to Bend, called the only person he knew there, and asked for the names of people who could give him information on the local job market, employers, the economic state of the area, and so on. Through referrals, he expanded his contact list; he spoke to 60 people by phone or in person within 10 days.

Doug worked in Bend for a year as Assistant Controller of a manufacturing company. When the owner stepped down after an incapacitating stroke, Doug accepted an offer from an attorney in Bend who asked Doug to join his solo practice. "That's where I got my first real taste of lawyering," says Doug. At the firm, he felt extremely fortunate to be working with Craig Edwards. "He was a man of incredible integrity," Doug comments. "He had a sense of humor. He was not a workaholic. He was known as a man of integrity and intelligence in the community. He was the perfect person for me to practice law with."

Doug's interest in business was still brewing, however. It wasn't that he disliked law practice. "My qualm with the practice of law," Doug explains, "is that I don't want to take from the economy but rather to give something to it, as a manufacturer does. I was interested in business because I wanted to produce goods, to provide something of economic benefit to the community rather than a service, as in a law or accounting firm."

In 1994, while still at the law firm, Doug was approached by former classmate Steve Bryan and offered a job as Controller of Pierian Spring, which had already enjoyed substantial early success. The fit with his business interests was ideal, and he accepted the offer. Now Doug thrives on the dynamic nature of the manufacturing sector, particularly the rapidly evolving software industry. He notes, "Work is all about solving problems, most of which turn into opportunities. And you can do it with a sense of humor."

Of his working relationship with Steve, Doug says, "It's a pleasure to work with someone with the same background. There is no pretense to our relationship; he's been down the exact same road. We don't owe each other any false deference. It's a fun environment."

When Doug describes the qualities he admires in professional colleagues, one dominant theme emerges: integrity. "Craig Edwards and Steve Bryan embody good, successful people of integrity," says Doug. "If you have that, everything else will fall into place. You will be concerned not only with your employees but for your community. You will make decisions that are best for all parties. All other positive qualities stem from integrity." Is integrity such a rarity in our society? Doug thinks so. "Integrity can't be taught," he comments. "It's not a set of codes or canons . . . and you can't teach it in law school."

Doug's advice to those considering a career in law focuses on communication skills, particularly as they are honed in law school. "It's a tremendously powerful skill to be able to probe for information and dissect conversations. But law students need to be able to open communication between people rather than shut it down by putting people on the defensive. Not being able to temper the use of that probing and dissecting skill will be a detriment to personal success."

Doug's career, with all of its twists and turns, has allowed him to follow his dreams just as single-mindedly as Steve has pursued his goals. Both now find that their educational backgrounds and technical skills are providing them with an opportunity to contribute to the larger society in a meaningful way while achieving fulfillment in their own lives.

KEEP THEM SMILING—
A CONTRACT ATTORNEY'S CREED

Suzi Cohen . . .

CURRENT JOB:

Contract Lawyer (San Francisco)

CAREER HIGHLIGHTS:

Suzi Cohen was a pioneer of sorts when she became a contract attorney in 1983. Contract lawyering was rare at that time and few considered it a viable or desirable career path. But customer service and client relations skills had always been among Suzi's greatest strengths, and she built upon these talents to create a very successful practice—a practice where lawyers are her clients.

Suzi Cohen often feels she has experienced it all during her 13 years as a contract attorney. She has worked from home—dressed in pajamas and communicating with clients via phone, fax, and modem. On occasion, she has found herself sharing a small cubicle with a bookkeeper, and she has sometimes struggled with an uneven cash flow. As an independent contractor, she has also been able to move from project to project before boredom set in, has been included in fun events that would not otherwise have been accessible to her, and has enjoyed opportunities to work with fascinating clients and cases.

After graduating in 1977 from the University of Santa Clara School of Law in northern California, Suzi spent the next six years working as a litigator for three small law firms in northern and southern California. Generally, her experiences in these firms were not pleasant. In the late 1970s, the number of women litigators was still small. Because Suzi was the only woman lawyer in each of the three firms, she found her relationships with the other attorneys were often uncomfortable. In one firm, she was treated as an outsider, given little respect, and never included in business discussions nor invited to lunch with the other attorneys nor spoken to unless to be given an assignment.

Suzi realized these three working situations were tolerable only because of her strong relationships with most clients. Client relations and customer service had always been among her strong points; prior to law school she had worked for nine years for the local telephone company in Los Angeles as a customer service manager. Deciding that she wanted to use her client relations skills, set her own schedule, be involved in a variety of issues, and be respected for her work, Suzi left her third firm in 1983 to begin working as a contract attorney. Her decision made her somewhat of a pioneer. Contract lawyering, which is a burgeoning field today, was relatively rare in 1983. In fact, general thinking at that time was that good lawyers did not hire themselves out to other lawyers.

Now lawyers are Suzi's clients. They hire her by the hour to handle their overflow work and to benefit from her expertise in litigation analysis and preparation. Her fine work, excellent customer service, and superior ability to cultivate meaningful and harmonious relationships with her clients are finally being given the accolades and respect those talents deserve. A number of Suzi's clients have used her services for years and continue to give her more work. Obviously she is doing something right.

What she loves best about her work as a contract attorney is the opportunity to venture into a new legal area—to become immersed in the law and "come up to speed" and then cleverly use her skills to move her lawyer-client to a successful position on the case. Suzi finds that additional benefits of her contract practice include —

- earning a decent income on an hourly basis without the pressure, rampant in almost all law firms, to produce billable hours;

- working flexible hours that provide time for personal life choices;

- experiencing the challenge of picking up a new file and quickly delving into the basic information necessary for the assignment;

- having responsibility for only a portion of a case or for just one project rather than having to track a case for many years;

- working with an interesting variety of people and cases;

- experiencing the intellectual challenge—on an almost daily basis—of examining diverse legal issues;

- working in a home office outfitted for instant communication with her established clientele; and

- having control over who the "boss" is by choosing which attorneys to work for.

But there are drawbacks. The quantity of available work fluctuates, causing irregular income and creating the need to budget carefully. In addition, all of Suzi's taxes, health and disability insurance, and vacation and sick time are self-paid. Although she can refuse cases and clients, Suzi nevertheless sometimes finds herself working with disorganized attorneys, with terrible management systems, who wait until the last minute to call her. She also encounters "sloppy" attorneys who have not thought through their long-term case strategy—attorneys she must tactfully educate. Worse yet are attorneys who refuse "to listen to the law" when it clearly is against their case—attorneys who expect Suzi to support their predetermined answers whether or not the law does.

According to Suzi, she has had to confront some additional issues in order to feel comfortable as a contract attorney. For example, she has had to recognize that her own ego cannot always be in the forefront if she is not the decision-maker on a case. At times she has had to forgo all control over an approach and case strategy—although many of her long-time clients trust her judgment and consult with her when making strategy decisions. To be an effective contract attorney, Suzi has had to become an individual who is equally at ease walking into a new office—with new people, a new case, and new issues—or being dropped into the middle of an existing case. Moreover, she has occasionally had to chase slow-paying attorneys. In fact, Suzi was once paid with several dirty, disintegrating $100 bills that even a bank would not accept. She did later collect her fee, but she no longer works for that lawyer.

Any drawbacks are balanced by the interesting and often humorous incidents Suzi has encountered in her travels to many law offices. For instance, in one of the largest cases on which she has worked, a multi-million dollar libel case with more than 100 witnesses, she was responsible for issuing all subpoenas, then marshalling and controlling all witnesses over a period of several months. A number of the witnesses were cowboys. Because their date for appearance at trial changed daily, she spoke to them and to their families so often that she became privy to their histories, their celebrations, and even their drinking problems, learning which ones needed to be watched closely and which could be trusted to appear without a "designated driver." In another case, Suzi was hired to assist on a trial quite far into trial preparation. During a conference on the case in the judge's chambers, and after hearing some of Suzi's remarks and analysis, the judge commented to the lead attorney that he should have brought her into the case sooner.

As a contract lawyer, Suzi credits her success in obtaining and retaining clients to the same client relations skills she has exhibited since the beginning of her legal career. She says, "I make each client feel they are top priority—the most important client—and make each project like my own. I am also absolutely timely in completing my projects so that my clients never have to worry about whether we will miss a deadline." And, if Suzi is no longer working on a particular case, she always contacts her attorney-client to learn the results of the work she has performed, both for her own education and to indicate her continuing interest in the case and its issues.

Suzi, who has a very quick wit and a wonderful sense of humor, asserts that her good relationships with her clients are a result of "adapting my interpersonal style to mesh well with my client's style." She adds, "I use a lot of humor and find it to be the best ulcer preventative and the best way to get along with clients." Her motto could be "keep them smiling and they come back for more."

When Suzi is thrown into a case with unfamiliar law, she informs the hiring attorney of her lack of expertise in that particular area and lets the attorney decide if she should take on the project. She was recently brought into a pending case just months before trial and was asked to prepare a complex motion for summary judgment utilizing volumes of depositions in an unfamiliar area of the law. After acknowledging her lack of experience in the subject area, she was given the green light by her attorney-client. As to her comfort level in such a situation, she comments: "You bite down that moment of fear and initial panic and just get on with it."

In fact, new law and issues arise on a regular basis. Contract attorneys are often called upon to handle all kinds of novel legal and factual situations on a moment's notice. That is both the terror and the thrill for those who make their living doing contract work.

LITIGATOR DISCOVERS UNBEATABLE COMBINATION

Jay G. Trezevant . . .

CURRENT JOB:

Lead Trial Attorney, Felony Bureau, Hillsborough County State Attorney's Office

CAREER HIGHLIGHTS:

Jay Trezevant has discovered he possesses a talent and a passion for trying cases. A wheelchair-bound attorney, Jay is following a career path he had once thought impossible due to his disability. He credits his success, at least in part, to the fact that he loves his job. "If you're bright, work hard, and do what you enjoy, you can't be beat," he says, "but being bright and working hard isn't always enough. Sooner or later you're going to come up against someone who has all three, and then they'll have the advantage."

After having spent four years as a corporate tax attorney, Jay Trezevant has found his niche as the Lead Trial Attorney in the Felony Bureau of the Hillsborough County State Attorney's Office. Now he spends most of his days doing the one thing he had ruled out as a law student—litigating jury trials.

Jay, who describes himself as very pragmatic, decided in high school that he would pursue a law degree after talking to many successful business persons who said that they wished they had studied law. His commitment to law school intensified after he broke his neck in a diving accident when he was a high school senior, leaving him a quadriplegic. "I saw developing my intellect and academic credentials in a specialized area as an equalizer to lessen the effect of my physical impairment," Jay comments. He decided to seek an accounting degree, a law degree, and then a Master of Laws in Taxation because he thought a specialized transactional practice would be the most practical for a wheelchair-bound attorney.

Adhering to his plan, Jay graduated from the University of Florida's School of Accounting with honors and immediately enrolled in Florida's joint degree program to earn his master's degree in accounting concurrently with his Juris Doctorate from the College of Law. Although he never enjoyed accounting, he loved law school and likened reading cases to reading "short stories." Because he had concluded that he would never do trial work, he avoided criminal law and trial practice—focusing instead on tax and transactional courses. After graduation, Jay spent one semester as an adjunct professor teaching Business Law at the College of Business and then returned to the College of Law to earn his LL.M. in Taxation.

Jay interviewed for, and was offered, a prestigious clerkship with the Tax Court in Washington, D.C. Unfortunately, due to the relatively low salary and the costs associated with his special needs, he had to turn down the opportunity. Ultimately, he chose to join a well-respected sole practitioner who specialized in tax and corporate law in hopes of assuming greater responsibility early in his career. Although Jay was able to work on significant matters, it didn't take long for him to realize that the large corporations for whom he was working would never become his personal clients. Jay decided that going out on his own and developing his own client base was his next move. Returning to his hometown, he began his practice with an emphasis on corporate, tax, and trusts and estates.

Once he got his practice going, Jay began to recognize the tremendous value of trial experience. He started to wonder if he might have erred by not giving trial work a chance. Jay knew his strong interpersonal skills would serve him well as a trial lawyer—but, in law school, he had focused on what he thought would work rather than assessing what he would be good at. He had also been concerned about whether or not he would be able to work long hours and generate the energy needed to control the courtroom. Now that he had a few years of practice behind him, Jay felt more confident and decided to go talk to the State Attorney and see if there might be an opportunity in his office.

Jay's fateful conversation with the State Attorney was four years, two promotions, and hundreds of trials ago. He now knows beyond a reasonable doubt that a wheelchair isn't necessarily a liability in the courtroom—and that it can even be an asset. "Sometimes I think my wheelchair and my reputation may intimidate the other side," he says. Jay claims he overcomes his impairment by being highly organized and working harder to make sure things go smoothly. He has an assistant—

usually a college or law student—who works with him. Together they organize, plan, and rehearse every aspect of each trial. As of the time he was interviewed for this book, Jay had never lost a felony trial—although he was quick to add, "My record could end next week."

Jay attributes his success at the State Attorney's Office, at least in part, to the fact that he loves his job. In fact, Jay asserts, "If you're bright, work hard, and do what you enjoy, you can't be beat—being bright and working hard isn't always enough. Sooner or later you're going to come up against someone who has all three, and then they'll have the advantage." For Jay, trying cases is incredible fun. "The unexpected happens all the time, and I enjoy the gamesmanship—thinking about what's wrong with the defense's story." He also shared that his most satisfying moments are during a trial when he knows that "it's working." He recalled a moment during a kidnapping case: "I looked at the victim during my closing argument, and I could tell that she knew that I had done all that I could do. That was very satisfying," he said, "and, of course, there is nothing like hearing that guilty verdict."

Although Jay is immensely satisfied with his current position, he continues to think ahead. "Right now my focus is on winning trials and having an employment record that is beyond reproach," Jay comments. Unlike many prosecutors, Jay seeks out media cases in hopes of furthering his reputation and his career. "I'd love to have the opportunity to work for the U.S. Attorney's Office someday," he says.

What advice does Jay have for law students and young lawyers? "Take the time, early on in your career, to figure out what you're good at and what you enjoy," he counsels. "There was so much I didn't understand about the practice of law as a law student. I should have given more thought to what I was good at and what I enjoyed . . . instead of focusing on what opportunities seemed reasonable."

YOU MAKE OF IT WHAT YOU PUT INTO IT...

Angela Hawekotte . . .

<u>CURRENT JOB:</u>

Partner, Adams & Hawekotte
(Pasadena, California)

<u>CAREER HIGHLIGHTS:</u>

Angela Hawekotte's first career move was to follow in the footsteps of her family's long line of certified public accountants—after she obtained her law degree. Her 5 1/2 years as a tax accountant paid off in the end. She has masterfully combined her talents in accounting, her desire to practice law, her superb writing skills, and several years of experience at an international law firm in the successful launch of her own practice. When it comes to making the best of the knowledge she has gained, Angela sums up the secrets to her success by saying, "You make of it what you put into it. . . ."

Angela's father was right. The Hawekotte family has an innate tendency for numbers. No matter how much she was intrigued by the idea of becoming a public defender, Angela's professional life seemed to steer her back into the world of accounting. She was certainly surrounded by it. Her father, a retired partner of Arthur Andersen & Co., was with the firm for 33 years. Her two older brothers and an uncle were CPAs at the company, too. She muses, "I think my family holds the record for having the most family work there at one time or another!"

With a mild demeanor, a sense of humor, and a constant, friendly smile, it's not hard to see why Angela can put at ease anyone who might be sitting in the same room with her. It is likely that these three attributes—and her insatiable love for learning—are what helped her glide through many years of discovery before settling down to practice law.

By the time she was in her second year at Loyola Law School, Angela started to think about what kind of law she wanted to practice. She liked criminal law, but she also liked tax law. Fortunately, she was saved from the need for an immediate decision by an opportunity to apply for a Rotary International fellowship for a year's study abroad. She was the first member of her local club in east Whittier, California, to apply. Competing against persons from other area clubs, she won and became the only woman in her district's history to receive a fellowship. With an undergraduate degree in political science and a particular interest in international affairs, Angela chose to study international law and relations at the University of Wales the following year.

At the end of her year of study, as she was preparing to return to California, she met a member of the British Parliament. She was offered a short-term job to work with Parliament members Geraint Howells and David Alton (now Chief Whip of the Liberal Democrats) at the Houses of Parliament in London. That brief assignment stretched to an entire parliamentary year (October 1980 through July 1981). Angela had a wonderful experience writing speeches and giving tours of the Houses of Parliament. "I even argued a final appeal before the Social Securities Commission of Britain," she reminisces. "I lost, but it was a good experience."

It would have been easy for Angela to continue living and working in England, but she knew it was time to return to the States and pursue her law career. With a leaning toward tax law, she decided to look for firms with a tax practice. She took her father's advice and talked to the head of the tax division at Arthur Andersen, also an attorney. When she met Russ Lippman, he told her that for some time he had been thinking about hiring more lawyers into public accounting because their background is very helpful.

By the end of their meeting, Angela was offered a job. Russ liked her résumé, and she was convinced the job was a very good way to learn all about tax. Angela attended night school to supplement the accounting courses she had already taken and eventually passed the CPA exam. During her tenure at Arthur Andersen, she learned about almost every area of tax: estates, utilities, manufacturing, international, and oil and gas.

It wasn't long after Angela started her search for a law firm with a tax practice that New York-based Whitman & Ransom (now Whitman Breed Abbott & Morgan) offered her a position—they were looking for a lawyer with an accounting background. Although law firm life was an adjustment for Angela, who had been out of law school for eight years, she took the ball and ran with it. While at the firm, her focus was tax and corporate law. However, when the need arose for an associate to learn the highly specialized area of municipal finance law, she tackled that, too—and well.

After four years at Whitman & Ransom, Angela was ready to take the plunge and open her own practice. Her motivation arose partly from her entrepreneurial spirit and partly from the need for a flexible schedule after her first son was born. Since that time, it has not simply been luck that Angela's practice has thrived more with each year.

With a concentration in the areas of taxation, estate planning, and corporate law, Angela's tax background has always been useful. Her knowledge of taxes, she says, comes into play with almost everything she does. "Often times I think of things other lawyers may not think of just because I have that perspective," she comments. "I'm lucky that a number of people come to me because I have both backgrounds."

As a member of the Pasadena and Los Angeles bar associations, the Rotary Club, and other business groups, Angela has developed an excellent networking system. Through these organizations, she has made many friendships and business contacts, and much of her work comes to her by word of mouth. She adds that other lawyers are her greatest source of referrals. Because she has gotten to know lawyers with different practice specialties, she and her colleagues often refer business back and forth.

Angela firmly believes in the importance of lawyers joining bar associations and other business groups—and thinks it's a mistake not to participate in professional organizations. "It is invaluable," she stresses, "to bounce ideas off of one another and avoid the need to reinvent the wheel." She likes to remind others that memberships in such groups also help to develop social skills. "It's important to remember that our law business is about dealing with human beings and communicating on a personal level."

John Park, president of BB World Corporation, has been Angela's client for 10 years and has great trust in her as his attorney. He became her regular client when his previous attorney, a partner from Angela's former law firm, moved to San Diego. The long distance commute made regular meetings difficult, so John chose to remain with Angela. He can vouch for the fact that she practices what she preaches: "She is very competent," he says without hesitation. "I feel very comfortable talking to her and admire that she is always thinking about her client—not only business."

It is Angela's feeling that people sometimes go into the law profession with the wrong expectations. She remarks that making a lot of money was a thing of the eighties. Angela adds, "You have to recognize that and be willing to enter a service profession that intrigues you and entices you to learn new areas all the time—and to solve problems. If that is your bent, you will love it—and always will."

FROM NURSE TO LAWYER TO POLITICIAN

Mavis Thompson . . .

CURRENT JOB:

Circuit Clerk, City of St. Louis (St. Louis, Missouri)

CAREER HIGHLIGHTS:

Mavis Thompson grew up in a community of extended family members who supported her every success and encouraged her to pursue her greatest dreams. She has enjoyed success as a nurse, a lobbyist, a Public Defender, and now as an elected public official. She was the first female—indeed, the first African-American—to hold a St. Louis city-wide elected office, in a city with a minority population over 50%. As Circuit Clerk, she supervises the state courts within St. Louis, supervising 250 employees in 31 divisions. She strives to manage the challenges of being an African-American and a woman in a field—politics— that has been known as inhospitable to both.

Mavis Thompson always wanted to be a nurse. Her childhood heroine was Julia, an African-American nurse played by Dihann Carroll on a popular 1960s television show of the same name. Mavis realized that initial dream, earning her B.S. in nursing, and worked in several hospitals in her native St. Louis. She then moved to Washington, D.C., and became a certified OB/GYN nurse at Georgetown University Medical Center. Following this position, she remained in the nation's capital as a lobbyist on Capitol Hill on behalf of patient care rights for the Washington, D.C., Professional Nurses Association. In her forays to Capitol Hill on behalf of the nurses' group, she was frequently told, "Oh, you don't know the law." She was undeterred. "I often found myself researching issues in the law library," she comments.

Her interest in law had been sparked. "I said to myself, 'OK, I can do this,'" Mavis recalls. She returned to Missouri to attend the University of Missouri-Columbia School of Law, envisioning that her specialty would be "medical malpractice law, health law, or risk management— something that related to both degrees."

Of her time in law school, Mavis says, "I had a good experience in law school. I was one of those crazy people who actually liked law school. But law school is not an easy decision. It's one the most challenging curriculums." Throughout law school, Mavis worked two 12-hour shifts as a nurse each weekend. She says of herself, "I wasn't the best of students, but I was a good student. I was well-rounded." Mavis was active and served in several leadership positions in the Black Law Students Association, the Board of Advocates, and the Student Bar Association.

Among the benefits of attending law school, Mavis cites the diverse career options available. She worked for a medical malpractice firm while in school and found her interests changing from health care to trial work. After graduation, she took a position as a Public Defender in St. Louis, which she enjoyed tremendously. She especially valued the experience she gained in court during her three years there. At that time, Mavis also began exploring an interest that would become a dominant role for her later: politics. She ran for State Representative in 1992. She says, "After law school, I was active in my neighborhood and ward. I thought I could do a good job as a State Rep." She barely lost the election. "That got my juices boiling for politics," she recalls.

A year later, Mavis campaigned on behalf of the man who became the first African-American mayor of St. Louis. When he won the election, he vacated his elected position as Circuit Clerk in the court system. He recommended to the Governor that Mavis be appointed to serve the remaining year of his term; she was also endorsed by several local organizations and was appointed. Running a campaign to keep the position a year later, Mavis was elected on her own merits. She was the first African-American female—and, in fact, the first female—elected official in St. Louis, a city with a minority population over 50%.

Of her political success, Mavis says, "Personally, I never saw myself in politics. But, looking back, other people saw the political potential in me before I saw it in myself." Mavis had always taken leadership positions and freely voiced her passion over issues of importance to her. Perhaps politics was just the logical evolution of her career.

As the Circuit Clerk, Mavis explains, "My job is to supervise the state courts within St. Louis. They include criminal courts, civil courts, and family courts. I supervise 250 employees in 31 divisions." Her staff handles administrative tasks such as collecting child support payments and handling initial filings in lawsuits. The work is a good fit for Mavis. "I love my job immensely," she says. "It's a very people-oriented job, and I'm a people person." At the end of her term in 1998, she plans to run for re-election.

Being an elected official has its own challenges. Mavis takes very seriously the moral component of her job. "I run a very large public office," she comments. "I am an elected official. There is a fine line between balancing public resources and having a political position. You always want to be above board so you are not compromising the public trust." There is also a very human side to being an elected official that must be handled with sensitivity to people's needs. "As an elected official people don't look at me as just the Circuit Clerk," Mavis explains. "If my neighbor wants to report that her trash hasn't been picked up, she calls me."

Mavis is motivated by knowing her work has meaning beyond her own career satisfaction. She comments, "What drives me is making a difference here on this earth. In my community, or city, or nation, what impact can I have?" Her community involvements include serving on the boards of several organizations and engaging in public speaking, particularly to young people.

Mavis is also motivated by a profound debt to what she describes as her "village." She paraphrases an African proverb—"It takes a village to raise a child." Mavis comments, "We've gotten away from that here in the U.S." She adds, "I come from a lower middle-class, African-American family. I was the first one to graduate from high school, although my parents finished their high school education when I was in college." She also enjoyed the enormous support of her close-knit extended family and cites an example: "My church and neighborhood sent three bus loads of people to attend my graduation from nursing school!"

Perhaps the greatest challenge Mavis has faced comes from the fact that she has often been the only one who was "different" among a group of homogeneous people. Her parents and grandparents encouraged her involvement in activities, but she was frequently the only child of color. "I felt pressure to represent my race," says Mavis. "It was a burden." Some things have never changed. She continues to be challenged by what she calls the "isms"—sexism and racism. "It's mostly covert, sometimes overt," she explains. She adds, "Some people are tiring of the race issue, but that's part of my life every day. Store clerks follow me around all the time. It's difficult finding panty hose in my shade." In law school Mavis had thought her life would change. "We're older now—we're professionals—I won't experience racism," she had told herself. "But," she says, "it was there, just more covert."

In looking back at her career, Mavis sees a lot of value in having a law degree, even though she is not a traditional lawyer. "Law teaches you to be analytical and to anticipate the other side's point of view," Mavis comments. "It is very intense." She adds, "A certain amount of arrogance goes with being an attorney—a 'Type A' personality. You need a drive toward solving problems and getting people the information they need." Mavis' satisfaction comes from being able to provide those services to people around her.

Outside the office, Mavis likes to read, go to the theater, listen to music, and shop. She has successfully bridged the gap between being an effective professional who serves in a highly visible public role and not losing sight of the public whom she serves.

On the Dual Career Track

Eric Kearney . . .

As President of the Student Bar Association at the University of Cincinnati College of Law, Eric Kearney was asked to deliver remarks at the hooding ceremony for his class. He paused a moment when he arrived at the podium and then carefully wove every person, by name, into his speech. Eric's unique ability to grasp and relate to the individual challenges faced by others has helped him succeed as a well-respected attorney with concentrations in commercial litigation and small business development—and as the publisher of the largest African-American monthly magazine in Ohio, Indiana, and Kentucky.

Eric meets his clients wearing a well-tailored suit and his signature bow tie. His youthful appearance is quickly put aside in favor of a soft-spoken and unassuming voice that draws the listener to him. He is currently a United States Bankruptcy Court Panel Trustee and a partner with Cohen, Todd, Kite and Stanford in Cincinnati. He spent five years as an associate with Strauss & Troy before joining Cohen, Todd in 1994. In 1995, Eric and his wife, Jan-Michele Lemon, also a practicing attorney, purchased *NIP (News, Information & Pictures) Magazine.*

Eric has been recipient of the *Applause! Magazine* Emerging Leader Award and the YMCA Black Achiever Award—evidence that his contributions to the community have not gone unnoticed.

Eric traces his decision to pursue a career in law to a time when he witnessed domestic violence in his third-grade classroom. The incident forced him to look outside of his world at the things that were happening around him. Eric's listening skills have been a key to his success, as has his willingness to become involved in efforts to change behaviors and situations to enhance the quality of life of others. His person-to-person skills help him structure relationships with clients that promote effective problem solving.

In addition to his accomplishments as an attorney and publisher, Eric has served on numerous boards, has written for the local newspaper, and has been named one of the "top 40 business leaders under 40." Where does Eric's energy come from? What motivates him? When does he sleep?

"I think it's important to have a career or an avocation outside of the law," Eric says. "Owning a business has helped me to understand the needs of the clients better." As an undergraduate at Dartmouth, Eric always thought he would work in the private sector and eventually run for political office. At different points in his life, he has wanted to be a writer, an architect, and an actor. "Undergrad was very difficult for me, so I was relieved to find that I enjoyed most parts of law school," Eric comments when asked about his aspirations. "Law school was more complex and demanding than I thought, so I became more pragmatic about my career. Since law school, my experience has been that things take much longer than I thought and are more difficult." In 1993, Eric ran unsuccessfully for Cincinnati City Council. His comments about this experience reflect his ability to find the positive in most things that he does. "Running for City Council was terrible for my legal career," he says, "but enabled me to meet new people and learn new things."

Eric has continued to accept such new challenges as serving on the boards of social service agencies, hosting his own monthly cable television show, and continually enhancing his law practice. His ability to listen—to digest and assimilate information—creates the impression that he is always trying to solve a problem. Eric reaches out in a warm and caring way to everyone he meets. He consistently builds stores of information that enable him to meet future challenges head on. He generally sleeps only four or five hours a night and is motivated by what he accomplishes in the other 20 hours to continue this routine.

When Eric is in the front of a courtroom, he remembers what he learned in law school. "I think about what it means to be a lawyer," he says of his court appearances. "It's not always your legal skills that will win the case but the dynamics of the relationships that you have built within the system. Being a runner and law clerking were very good jobs that gave me knowledge and experience about the practical aspects of the law."

Eric's career goal when beginning as a first-year law student was to "do well academically and obtain a good education." Now he derives satisfaction from challenging existing laws. When asked what he has had to overcome to follow his chosen career path, Eric answers, "Inspiring confidence in my work and my abilities is a constant challenge." He also takes a minute to reflect on his colleagues and to note that those he most admires are "people who seem so know what they want to do, people who are genuinely happy and content, and people who have obtained a high degree of expertise and who are knowledgeable." These are the people that Eric sees as successful.

"I thought that I would be motivated by money," Eric replies when asked to think back to his law school concepts of success. "Being in a law firm seemed to be 'the thing' when I was in law school." Clerkships played a part in helping him decide what he would do when he began law practice in 1989.

Eric appears consistently motivated by what he can contribute through his knowledge of the law and his expertise in problem solving. He quietly takes on responsibility and challenges and looks for the lesson that will enable him to help the next person in an even more effective and timely manner. His experience in third grade motivated him to listen, to assimilate information, and then to find a way to act on the information with a positive and educational approach.

Eric may claim that inspiring confidence in his work and his abilities is a "constant challenge," but people who meet him instantly know that this successful attorney and business person is quite capable of handling the challenges that await around the next corner.

SOMETHING DIFFERENT EVERY DAY...

Tom Condon . . .

CURRENT JOB:

Columnist Reporting on
Urban Affairs for
The Hartford Courant
(Hartford, Connecticut)

CAREER HIGHLIGHTS:

A native of New London, Connecticut, Tom Condon has stayed close to home to write about the people of Connecticut and the issues that affect their daily lives. His legal education has provided him with a "window into how things work" in both civil and criminal matters, and he uses this knowledge on a daily basis to write about the needs of the community. Always looking for a story, he finds his work offers "something different every day."

Tom Condon recalls that the great Babe Ruth once said, "You mean they're going to pay me to play ball?" For Tom, writing is like playing ball. . . . It sustains and motivates him.

Tom was a journalist even before he attended law school. During his college years at Notre Dame, he enjoyed reading and writing and was involved in the school newspaper and radio. After graduating in 1968 with a degree in English, he worked part-time for the *Washington Daily News*. One weekend while attending a wedding in Connecticut, he walked into *The Hartford Courant* and landed a full-time job as a reporter. However, after only three months on the job, Tom was on his way to Vietnam, where he served as an Army Lieutenant in military intelligence. *The Courant* held his job for him, so he was able to return full-time to *The Courant* after his service.

The son of a lawyer and probate judge, Tom decided to follow in his father's footsteps and enroll in law school. He attended the evening division of the University of Connecticut School of Law while working during the day as a general assignment reporter for *The*

Hartford Courant. Holding down a full-time job while going to law school was not easy. Tom could be covering a story anywhere either in or out of the state of Connecticut on a given day—often having to drive clear across the state to get back to the newspaper office in time to run to class. He remembers one particularly busy day when he was assigned to cover a story at the United Nations in New York City. He was able to get the story and return to Hartford in time to attend the second half of a law class.

Tom devoted weekends to study as well as studying whenever possible during the week. He recalls his schedule as "brutal," but he felt fortunate that he did not have family obligations in addition to his job like so many others in his class. Getting a law degree and working at the same time means putting the rest of one's life on hold, according to Tom. After graduation from law school, Tom continued to work at *The Courant*, but he worked nights so he could spend his days as a lawyer for Neighborhood Legal Services for a year. He also practiced solo for a time. While in law school, Tom had felt a lot of pressure to practice law. Working as a lawyer, however, he soon realized "that's them, and I'm me. I like to go down to the office and write."

Today, Tom writes three columns a week for *The Courant* and appears two times a week on Channel 30 in Hartford, where he presents his commentary live. Tom is well known among the newspaper's readers, and people look forward to reading what he has to say. He particularly likes to comment on local issues, and he often relies on his ability to understand legal language and analyze legal issues to bring depth and scope to his work. In addition to writing, Tom does his share of public speaking; he frequently moderates panel discussions sponsored by local organizations, including the bar association.

Much of Tom's writing addresses community topics that are related to legal issues in some way. Once his knowledge of complicated zoning codes was helpful in a Hartford case that involved developers who were constructing housing on land in the middle of city blocks. Because these buildings were built in inaccessible places, which was dangerous for security and for fire and police protection, something needed to be done. Tom's well-written articles focused public attention on the zoning problem and contributed to changing the zoning regulations to make living in these areas safer for everyone.

When Tom is not writing about community issues, he is writing about people. Ideas for his columns and stories come from letters people write to him, from telephone calls from sources he has cultivated, and from following the news. He has written about bad nursing homes, crooked towing operators, problems related to transportation and public housing, and welfare policy issues. Tom writes with authority because he understands regulations; he knows how things work and how changes get accomplished.

Human interest stories are also favorite topics. Once he wrote about a dance teacher who volunteered to teach ballroom dancing to inner city children after school. Another of Tom's most interesting assignments was a magazine piece he wrote about Richard LaPointe, a mentally retarded man from Manchester, Connecticut, who was convicted of rape and murder and whose story aired on *60 Minutes*. After the story appeared on television, Tom heard from the family of another victim who was raped three days after the 1989 murder/rape for which LaPointe was convicted. There are "striking parallels" in the two cases, and questions have been raised concerning the validity of some of the forensic evidence used in court to convict LaPointe. Tom continues to write about the case. He hopes that Dr. Henry Lee, who is head of the Connecticut state forensic laboratory and nationally known for his expertise on DNA testing, will take over the case.

Early in his career Tom's goal was to "develop as a writer by mastering the different forms—columns, feature stories, magazine articles, and books." Today, Tom is an accomplished writer who has certainly mastered several different forms of expression. He is the author of a number of books: *The Executive Handbook of Humor—A Public Speaking Joke Book; Fire Me and I'll Sue; Age Discrimination;* and *Legal Lunacy—Humorous Laws and Ordinances.* His latest book, which was published in July 1996, is entitled *School Rights: A Parent's Legal Handbook and Action Guide.*

What does the future hold for Tom? He hopes to write a novel someday, and he may retool a short story he once wrote and submit it for publication. Low key about his many talents and his local fame, Tom believes that more lawyers should become entrepreneurs and go into business for themselves—or work for major corporations that need smart people to run them.

HELPING NON-PROFITS ACHIEVE THEIR MISSIONS

Lawrence C. Henze . . .

CURRENT JOB:

Vice-President, USA Group
Noel Levitz (Chicago)

CAREER HIGHLIGHTS:

Larry Henze was a nontraditional law student and is now a nontraditional lawyer. He entered law school in a part-time program at age 28, having already gained experience in fundraising, development, and research. Since graduating from law school, Larry has become a successful consultant. Combining his legal knowledge with his prior expertise, he has helped numerous institutions increase their marketing potential.

Although he doesn't practice law, Larry Henze frequently uses his law degree and is proud of the fact that he is a lawyer. He applied and was admitted to law schools when he was a senior at Carroll College in Waukesha, Wisconsin, but he was unable to attend at that time. Instead, he pursued a master's degree in Public Policy and Administration at the University of Wisconsin.

After working as a research analyst for the State of Wisconsin Division of Community Services, he returned to his *alma mater* to work in the development office. In January 1983, he was offered and accepted a position as Director of Annual Giving for the University of Wisconsin. He spent 3 1/2 years in that position and 3 1/2 years in corporate and foundation relations.

Despite his success in the field of development, Larry never lost sight of his dream of being a lawyer. In August 1983, he entered the University of Wisconsin Law School as a part-time student. He continued working full-time while attending law school part-time. Going to law school on a part-time basis was not easy and required an ability to juggle many conflicting demands. In addition to his full-time job, he had a wife and two children who also needed time and attention. As an indicator of the difficulty of attending law school part-time, of the 40 students who started in his class, only two finished as part-time students. Everyone else transferred to the full-time program or quit law school. Although the part-time program is structured to take six years, Larry finished the degree requirements in 5 1/2 years.

After graduating from law school in December 1988, Larry interviewed with law firms and looked at other opportunities. He decided to work with Ed Garvey at Sports Seminars, Inc. In conjunction with the University of Wisconsin, he started the Institute for Sports Representation and was the director of the first institute. Following this position, Larry returned to development work and accepted a job as Director of Development at the University of Dayton in Ohio. All of Larry's positions—both before and after law school—provided a rich background for his next career transition: a move into fundraising and legal consulting related to fundraising.

From March 1993 through September 1996, Larry was the president of Sigma Econometrics, a market research firm in Chicago that uses predictive modeling to identify customers or prospects. His clients included both commercial ventures and non-profit organizations. "One of my biggest achievements was building this startup company into a nationally recognized market research firm in the non-profit arena," Larry comments.

In September 1996, Larry joined USA Group Noel Levitz as a vice president with responsibilities in product development, marketing, and sales. USA Group Noel Levitz specializes in providing consulting and research services to the higher education market, and Larry is working to develop a predictive modeling service for enrollment management, retention, and fundraising.

Although he doesn't like the frequent travel required by his job, Larry particularly enjoys speaking to potential clients about how his company can help them achieve their goals. "I like my job so much because I'm able to help institutions achieve their missions through increasing their marketing potential," he says. The traits he admires the most in other people are commitment and dedication to ideals.

Outside of his job, Larry does volunteer work for the American Red Cross and the Arthritis Foundation. He also served as fundraising chair for his church's building campaign.

Larry has faced numerous obstacles, including serious medical problems and the deaths of both of his parents during the time he attended law school. He attributes his success to his "ability to keep looking to the future and not living in the past."

A Solo Practitioner with a Thriving Computer Consulting Business

David G. Sternlicht . . .

CURRENT JOB:

Solo Practitioner and Computer Consultant (New York City)

CAREER HIGHLIGHTS:

Having taken the risk of opening his own practice shortly after law school graduation, David Sternlicht is currently enjoying success in two professions: as a solo practitioner and as a computer consultant. David recommends self-employment to those who value freedom and control over their schedules but admits that being one's own boss requires stamina. As a lawyer, David is particularly proud to have won an Appellate court decision in a child support case he worked on over a period of four years.

David Sternlicht is at a crossroads. In some ways, he is a victim of his own success. As the president of a thriving computer consulting business, MACximize Consulting, and as a busy solo practitioner, David realizes he may soon need to decide which of his businesses will gain his undivided attention. In the meantime, as appropriate for this sometime actor, David enjoys juggling his multiple roles.

How David came to be a computer consultant/solo practitioner is a many-layered tale. As a law student and later as a recent graduate, David sampled law practice in a variety of settings, interning with two solo practitioners and a mid-sized New York City law firm. While David rates all of these experiences as positive and, in fact, encourages students to expose themselves to as many clinical opportunities as they can, his tenure with the solo practitioners seemed to resonate more deeply with him than his "big firm" experience.

As a law firm summer associate, David noticed the pressure to bill hours and the lack of client contact.

Now, as a solo practitioner, David particularly derives satisfaction from his ability to control his own schedule, to select only those clients and cases he feels he can handle effectively, and to see a case through from beginning to end. For David, independence is worth more than the salary a firm might offer. "If you're the type of person who's self-motivated, who has a flame burning inside you, and who enjoys the control and freedom of being your own boss, maybe solo practitice is right for you," David says. "I don't say become a solo practitioner—work less, make more money. Coming out of law school solo you may not make a lot of money, but you have a lot of control and that may be worth a lot more than money."

David's actual entrée into solo practice was influenced both by personal predilection and by the economic forces that were affecting the legal market when he graduated from Fordham University School of Law in 1991. No summer associates were extended offers of permanent employment at the firm where David spent his second-year summer. David rebounded by getting an associate offer from another respectably sized New York City firm shortly after graduation—only to have this firm dissolve. Doing pro bono work on behalf of battered women and the elderly and working part-time for a Connecticut solo practitioner, David continued to build his skills. But, after facing a year of underemployment following graduation, David felt a decision had to be made. "I couldn't have done it without the support of my wife actually," David explains. "You need someone there to say becoming a solo practitioner is a good idea because it's a crazy idea."

Concerned about his lack of practical experience, David nonetheless intuitively felt that becoming a solo practitioner was a good long-term investment, given the current instability of law firm life. (David points to classmates who held out longer than he did to get a law firm job only to find themselves in the marketplace again.) David took the plunge and opened shop in his apartment in March 1992, mindful of keeping operating costs low. Entrepreneurial and self-confident, David felt secure in his ability to attract clients by providing more personal attention at a lower cost than firms could offer. Technology enables him to operate without a support staff and, in a sense, is his support staff. Equipped with a computer, laser printer, fax machine, answering machines, and a pager, David is, as he says, an "accessible guy." His close proximity to the Fordham University School of Law library and LEXIS® covers his reference needs.

David credits his facility with the MacIntosh computer for enabling him to launch his solo practice efficiently. This facility also helped him survive those "quiet times" he encountered at the beginning of his solo practice venture and, unexpectedly, led to the development of his second business venture, MACximize Consulting.

When prospective cases were slow coming in at first, David advertised in local newspapers; however, he was disappointed by the quality of clientele attracted. David was getting some case referrals through relatives and friends but needed to augment his income. He did so by temping as a highly skilled secretary. Realizing his computer skill was such that he could not only do but also teach, troubleshoot, and repair, David entered into a computer consulting partnership with a law school colleague. When the partnership dissolved, David launched his own computer consulting company, and these activities have expanded to the point where—by a slim margin—most of David's time and income are now devoted to and derived from this business.

At the same time, David's case referral network and reputation have improved as former classmates, other attorneys, and solo practitioners from out of state now regularly pass cases along, making formal "advertising" unnecessary. Hence David's dilemma as he rushes from court to legal clients to computer clients—from research and writing to "surfing" the Internet and downloading updates for a computer program. David packs in a full day as he switches back and forth from his computer hat to his legal hat, and he sometimes wonders if his sanity will survive the process. Yet he seems reluctant to cast aside either business because he derives distinct satisfactions from both. "I try to put off that decision as much as possible while I'm still doing a good job at both," David says.

While computer consulting does not compare to the intellectual challenge of being an attorney, David finds it is in some ways a happier, less stressful profession. David compares the two professions this way: "Being a lawyer involves researching, writing, arguing, and waiting. And then you could still lose (the case). Being a computer consultant, if something is broken, I go in, I fix it, the client is happy, I'm done, I get paid. So it's different."

Although solo practitioners are sometimes advised to "specialize" in an area of the law, David finds this approach economically impractical for most beginning solo practitioners. David is honest with clients if he lacks expertise in a given area. However, he comments: "If I think that your case is a winner and I believe in it and you seem like the type of client that I'd like to deal with, I'll probably take your case." David advises beginning solo practitioners against taking on a lot of contingency cases because reimbursement may at best be eventual. Instead, he sometimes uses creative billing with clients (within bar association guidelines). For instance, David explains, "I may charge a certain amount based on an hourly rate and a certain amount based on contingency. I may take less later on if you pay me more up front; I may take more later if you pay me less up front."

Knowing when to consult others is essential yet can be awkward. David's contacts include friends at law firms, former law school and continuing legal education professors, and the bar association's legal referral numbers. He tries not to call anyone too often. However, David adds, "I try to use every resource I have because my best resource is other people's experience when I don't have my own." Successfully networking with the county clerk's office is also crucial to making certain that court papers are presented properly. Ironically, surviving the relative isolation of solo practice requires the strong people skills necessary to maintain a strong network of potential "helpmates."

If flexibility and propensity for risk led David to his current ventures, they may yet lead him to other uncharted waters in the future. But, in the meantime, David is happily, busily engaged in straddling the computer and legal worlds with skill and grace.

An Early Focus on Sports Law

Peter S. Roisman . . .

CURRENT JOB:

Director, Golf Division,
Advantage International, Inc.
(McLean, Virginia)

CAREER HIGHLIGHTS:

Ten years ago, Peter Roisman was a law student with a vision and a goal. Today he directs the Golf Division of a company representing athletes on four major continents. Peter credits his success in a highly competitive field to the fact that he never doubted he would someday be in sports law. He had known since the age of 10 that he wanted to be a lawyer—and as soon as he entered law school he knew he wanted to be a sports lawyer. Achieving success in his chosen field required more than desire, however. Determination, patience, creativity, knowledge, skill, and the support of a number of persons along the way have all been crucial to Peter's success.

Peter Roisman's advice to anyone who aspires to be a sports lawyer is, "As soon as you know what you want, go and get it. Don't hesitate. Don't allow doubts to influence you." Pointing to the number of people trying to get into the field, Peter adds: "Put 100% effort into your career. If you are thinking half-heartedly, then it's a waste of time." According to Peter, would-be sports lawyers need determination and a willingness to "pay the price." Other qualities he considers necessary for success include patience, dedication, creativity, knowledge of the market-place, knowledge of what a client's experience is, good legal and negotiating skills, writing and oral communication skills, people skills, and sales experience. All of these attributes enable a sports lawyer to do the best job possible for clients.

Peter's own path toward sports law began at an early age. A native of Hartford, Connecticut, Peter was active in sports such as soccer, baseball, golf, and basketball throughout grade school and high school. He can recall reading the sports page when he was only four years old. His father, who is also a lawyer and was once captain of his high school basketball team, was Peter's role model. Peter graduated from Amherst College in Massachusetts, where he participated in several intramural sports, was a four-year letter-earner on the golf team, and earned All-New England honors his senior season.

He applied to the University of Connecticut School of Law, was accepted, and was later granted a deferment for one year so that he could go to Florida to determine whether he would pursue playing professional golf. After only a few months, Peter realized that he did not want to play golf as a career. He wanted to represent athletes, but the year in Florida gave him a greater understanding of the things that are important to golfers.

Law school had been a logical choice for Peter, who comments, "I knew when I was 10 years old that I would be a lawyer." He didn't know then what type of lawyer he would be, but he comments, "As soon as I got to law school, I knew what I wanted to do." Peter is grateful for his early focus because he feels he didn't "lose any time." He attended the University of Connecticut School of Law because he considered it "an excellent school, offering a great financial advantage. It also offered a course with a professor, Lewis Kurlantzick, who knew about sports law."

Peter enrolled in the sports law course as soon as possible. An active participant in the sports law student group on campus, he also joined the National Sports Lawyers Association as a student member. Throughout law school, he traveled up and down the New England coast establishing a personal network as he met with professional athletes, coaches, representatives from such athletic equipment manufacturers as Spalding, and others in the sports field. He met John Toner, who was at that time Athletic Director at UCONN, and Jim Calhoun, the UCONN Huskies men's basketball coach. Peter also met Gordie Howe, a famous hockey player who lived in the Hartford area and played for the Hartford Whalers. Peter also attended many sports law conferences and read as much as he could find about the field and its practitioners.

In his second year of law school, Peter put together a large sports forum which was held at the school. Focusing on the issue of drug testing and privacy rights in athletics, the forum attracted major media attention and drew important people from the world of sports. Peter also got his first sports client in 1984, while he was still in law school.

When he graduated, Peter "hung his own shingle" and began practicing law—at first focusing much of his time on commercial matters. Occasionally he got referrals from his father. Because Peter had spent the previous four years building a network for himself in the sports world, he was now able to expand his contacts. Eventually, his practice grew to the point where he represented coaches and all-star athletes in baseball, hockey, and basketball.

"Everyone told me I was crazy," Peter says as he recalls those days when he was just starting out—everyone, that is, except his wife, his parents, a couple of close friends, and sports law professor Lewis Kurlantzick. People would tell Peter, "It's never been done—and certainly not in Hartford." To Peter, there was never a doubt. "Fortunately, my wife did support me in this endeavor," he notes and adds, "I lost money at this for several years."

A turning point in Peter's career came when one of his clients, Reggie Lewis, captain of the Celtics, died as a result of a heart problem. "It was a tremendously painful and devastating time in my life," Peter comments. "It shook me and hurt me in a lot of ways—emotionally, in both my heart and my head, and financially. It was really a struggle." That summer after Reggie's death Peter got a call from one of the managing directors of Advantage International who said that he understood how difficult Reggie's death was for Peter. Later that fall, the Advantage director called again and told Peter that Advantage anticipated an opening in the golf division. It was a big decision for Peter and for his wife Emily, who had just become a partner in a local law firm, to move from Hartford to Washington, D.C., with their two young children, but it seemed a good time for a move.

Today, Peter has come full circle, and his primary focus is again the sport of golf. Advantage International has four golf offices, which are located in Virginia, London, Australia, and Tokyo. Peter is also the National Secretary of the Sports Lawyers Association, the group he first joined as a student member. Peter thinks the best thing about his job is the opportunity to "work with the athletes who are striving to be the best in the world." Peter performs a valuable service. Despite the fact that his is a highly stressful job which places many demands on his time, Peter says, " . . . I love to go to work."

At present, Peter handles fewer than 10 clients personally. Typically he deals with anything from appearance and endorsement contracts to coordinating the financial management of some athletes with the financial planning division. His primary focus involves contract negotiations. Contract negotiations for individual sports athletes like tennis players and golfers often center around equipment and corporate sponsorships. "You have to get out there, get the sponsors, and put sponsorship deals together," Peter notes.

He feels very comfortable working at Advantage because the company's philosophy concerning negotiations meshes with his own personal philosophy. While Peter stresses the importance of doing the best job possible for every client, he comments, "You also have to realize that you are not trying to squeeze the very last nickel out of the people you are doing business with. Because if you make the negotiations so distasteful, they are not going to want to come back to you. We try to create fair deals which foster continuing relationships between clients and sponsors." Peter feels that a completely one-sided deal will ultimately hurt the client.

There are two very distinct kinds of "typical" days for Peter. On days when he is in the office and not on the road, he works from 8:30 a.m. to 8:00 p.m. It is not unusual for him to make a hundred telephone calls and receive the same number. He also writes as many as 20 letters and meets with his staff. Peter finds that he utilizes his legal background less and less because he can ask lawyers in the legal department to draft most documents. Instead, much of what Peter does now is sales—not only of himself and his company but also of his clients. Peter's travels may take him to any part of the world. Recently he went to India for a week to help develop the sport of golf in that country.

Peter laughs as he admits that his job is not always glamorous. It requires being willing to service the client and go the extra mile when necessary. More than once Peter has found himself taking calls on weekends or at 3:00 a.m., helping clients solve the more mundane problems of life that trouble us all. For example, he has even taken calls from a classified ad to sell a washing machine for a client. If it is a difficult time for the athlete, Peter tries to do whatever it takes. "You have to take it with a smile," he says.

Peter finds it hard to believe that only 10 years ago he was in law school. He sees himself doing different work ten years from now, but in the same field. He says he will probably be overseeing some of the things he has helped to build. He is looking forward to having more time to play golf again.

Peter attributes much of his success to the support of his family and others along the way. He comments, "It's hard to be successful without other people's support." He has always been a good team player who likes working with people. "It's a lot more rewarding," he says, "to do things together than by yourself."

SALES SKILLS CONTRIBUTE TO LEGAL SUCCESS

Diane Stehle Dix . . .

CURRENT JOB:

Associate, Thompson Hine & Flory, LLP (Cincinnati, Ohio)

CAREER HIGHLIGHTS:

Diane Stehle Dix spent five years in sales-related positions—winning national and regional awards for her sales efforts—before deciding to return to college to finish her undergraduate degree. She continued on to law school, wondering all the while about the wisdom of leaving a successful career behind for the uncertainties of the legal employment market. But today the skills Diane developed in her earlier career have helped her achieve success once again—this time as an attorney with a large law firm.

"My sales experience—running my own business and managing an active sales force, as well as training sales personnel—helped to prepare me for my position in a law firm," notes Diane Dix. Prior to attending law school, Diane spent six years in sales. One position as a regional manager included the responsibility of heading a national training team; another position as a sales manager for a local franchise required that she learn to interact with a wide range of people. Diane approached these sales positions determined to provide high quality customer service. Consequently, in one position she led the nation in sales, and in the other she was recognized with regional sales awards.

After six years in the workforce, Diane returned to college and finished her undergraduate degree in English, *Magna Cum Laude*. She then decided to continue on to law school. "I went to law school to learn a new craft and to develop analytical and writing skills," Diane explains. "I also felt that the practice of law would give me a sense of accomplishment and create career opportunities for me."

However, like many returning students, Diane sometimes questioned her future marketability, knowing she would be competing with younger graduates for job opportunities. "I certainly felt some self-doubt," she comments. "There are no lawyers in my family, and I was totally unfamiliar with the practice of law. As a returning student, I needed encouragement that I could do it!" Yet even in law school, Diane's upbeat and positive attitude and her ability to meet and greet new people were noticed and valued.

Diane actively pursued law clerk opportunities during her three years at the University of Cincinnati College of Law. "I expected to use my law degree working within a corporation or practicing corporate law with a focus on small businesses, although I was open to other possibilities," Diane explains. "My husband owned a business, and I was exposed to various legal, business, corporate, and employment issues," Diane adds. "I thought that a legal education would have very practical everyday application."

She spent the summer of her first year of law school and part of her second and third years working for a major bank in the Cincinnati area. Her easygoing manner combined with her determination to work hard earned her respect from her peers and recognition from the attorneys with whom she worked. "I became interested in banking, finance, and commercial law during law school," comments Diane. "I wanted to try private practice with a bank client and large corporate clients because I really liked the transactional work." As a law student with an interest in corporate coursework, she focused particularly on transactional courses and on a bankruptcy course taught by a local judge. Her law review article, which related to bankruptcy law, further enhanced the foundation she was building in this area. In addition, as an undergraduate English major, she had built research and writing skills.

Diane's legal interests were reinforced during her first position following law school, which was as a Law Clerk for a Judge with the United States Bankruptcy Court. "Because of my interest in business, I actively sought out attorneys in this area of practice," notes Diane. "I found that while I served as a Judicial Clerk for the Bankruptcy Court, I was meeting attorneys in the bankruptcy area whom I really respected."

Today, the same attributes that Diane sought in her sales career are the qualities she seeks to demonstrate as a lawyer. "Honesty, integrity, and follow-through—doing what you promise—are important," says Diane. "In sales, your customer expects that you will know your product and be there after the sale to provide support and direction. Effective attorneys are those who conduct their business in a civil and respectful manner, with a willingness to help one another and to assist each other in practice areas in which they have more or less experience."

As a successful sales manager, Diane developed very specific skills in managing the sale of her product and in training her support staff. Now she finds that many of these same skills are essential to her current position in a large law firm practicing in the corporate and bankruptcy areas. "I like the attention to detail that is part of my current position," Diane comments. She adds: "Precision is required in all transactional work. I love the interaction with clients and opposing counsel—and the interaction with more senior attorneys. I feel that I am always learning the law, but, at the same time, I am using my skills to improve. I am challenged by the idea of doing a project well. I like the fact that every project and the issues involved are different and unfamiliar, and that there are still aspects of the law that I need to learn."

Diane recognized early in her legal career that the responsibility for learning the profession is on her shoulders. She asks questions of the partners with whom she works and is conscious of her role in providing quality client service. Diane also volunteers her time, assisting with programs at the University of Cincinnati College of Law, and she is an active member of the school's Alumni Association Board of Trustees and of the Cincinnati Bar Association. Diane has learned that in order to be a successful attorney she must be willing to continue to share her expertise with those who are following her into the profession.

CRYSTAL CLEAR AMBITION

Janice L. Weis. . . .

CURRENT JOB:

Director, Environmental &
Natural Resources Law
Program, Northwestern School
of Law of Lewis and Clark
College (Portland, Oregon)

CAREER HIGHLIGHTS:

After graduating from law
school, Janice Weis went
directly into private practice
and developed a specialty in
environmental law. Six years
later, her expertise in the field
led to an exciting transition in
her legal career. She now
directs one of the country's
top university environmental
law programs. Returning to
the law school setting, Janice
now stands on the other side
of the lectern. Instead of
advising clients, she counsels
students, teaches, oversees a
full-time staff, and plans environmental conferences.

As children, many people think they know what they want to be when they grow up, but most end up doing something entirely different. This wasn't the case for Janice Weis. Janice not only knew that she was going to be a lawyer, she knew she would practice environmental law. At her high school reunion, she heard the same comment over and over: "Janice, you always knew you were going to be a lawyer—none of us are close to what we thought we would be doing!"

In junior high school, Janice loved participating in a mock trial presentation. After the program, her teacher suggested that she consider a law career, commenting that the field is made for people who like to argue without losing their temper and who enjoy writing. Although her parents thought she might be closing off options by making a career decision so early, she considered herself fortunate. "Because I knew what I was going to do," notes Janice, "I didn't spend a lot of time changing my major in college. I knew what I had to do to get there."

Janice's ambition was as crystal clear and focused as her energetic blue eyes. During high school, she worked one summer for the Youth Conservation Corps, spending months in the wilderness building trails. Her counselors were law students who encouraged her to combine advocacy skills with her interest in preserving the environment and developing sustainable uses of natural resources.

At the University of California, Hastings College of the Law, Janice took every environmental course possible. A lot of people advised her, however, that she should not expect to land an environmental job instantly after graduation. They told her she would have to pay her dues first by doing litigation or general transactional work. She was willing to do that, but she still knew what she wanted. So she concentrated on looking for firms with well-established environmental departments or practice groups. Somehow Janice knew in her heart that she wasn't going to stay in private practice forever, and she didn't necessarily want to wait for a firm to build up that practice.

Her persistence paid off. At the Riverside, California, law firm of Best, Best & Krieger, Janice was able to walk in the door and begin environmental work. Eric Garner, a partner at BB&K, interviewed Janice when she first came on board and worked closely with her for the next six years. He remembers a big water litigation case in northern California that required the trial team to live together in Hayward for nine weeks. The job demanded dedication and hard work. He recalls how Janice always kept her sense of humor during this period. "She is extremely talented," he says, "always fun to work with, and really seems to enjoy what she is doing."

In private practice, Janice received excellent training and honed her legal skills. A very detail-oriented person, she learned to craft documents precisely—sometimes revising a piece 10 or 20 times. She comments, "Documents that go to court have to be perfect. Memos to clients must have a certain look. I found myself very much in harmony with this system." Where some people detest this sort of tedium, she liked the creative process of knitting together cases that weren't exactly on point and finding ways they could be on point if particular arguments were made.

She also enjoyed going to court—the public arena part of the job—where she had to speak and think on her feet. "You can have a prepared speech," she says, "and you can have practiced and practiced and practiced, but you can't do that in court. The judge might let you talk for only two minutes or might have specific questions. You need to watch him or her and be very aware of what you are saying. I just loved that—I loved the adrenaline and the interaction."

As she sharpened her lawyering skills, Janice also displayed leadership abilities. When only a fourth-year associate, she co-chaired the firm's natural resources practice group. For three years she was a member of the Executive Committee of the California State Bar Environmental Law Section, and she was vice-chair of the Committee for one year. She also edited her firm's natural resources newsletter and authored two chapters of *California Water* (Solano Press, 1995).

Janice thoroughly enjoyed private practice. However, as her family started to grow and her research interests increased, she felt the need to make adjustments in her professional life. Her priorities as a lawyer didn't change, but her definition of success did. Success no longer meant working six or seven days a week. More simply, it meant being a good lawyer. When the position of Director of the Environmental and Natural Resources Law Program at Northwestern School of Law in Portland, Oregon, became available, Janice saw it as a great opportunity to blend her private practice background and her "people" skills. Garner of BB&K adds that the move was an excellent one for Janice: "She likes working closely with people and is a natural for this kind of work."

Life as a law school program administrator is indeed different. Students now take the place of clients for Janice. They stream in and out of her office throughout the day in need of advice or assistance. She finds counseling students and providing advice on important life decisions deeply satisfying. Janice also spends a lot of time on the telephone talking to prospective students. In addition, she meets with faculty to plan the program curriculum, plans for her class lectures, and organizes annual environmental conferences. On a busy day in private practice, she could easily have her secretary hold all calls in order to meet deadlines. At Northwestern, however, that is no longer the case— direct interaction with students is her job.

Janice reminds students that there are ways to help ensure success in the legal world. "Have a base to keep track of," she says. Her base was environmental law. Janice attributes her success to choosing a field in which she has a great deal of interest—a field she genuinely enjoys. "That is what keeps people motivated. If a person chooses an area where there are a lot of jobs, but in which he or she has no interest, that decision can lead to job dissatisfaction."

While in the law firm environment, Janice learned organizational and management skills to cope with the hard work and long hours. "Now," she says, "even the hardest thing here at the law school is such a pleasure!"

SUCCESS IS BEING A GOOD PROBLEM SOLVER

Kathryn A. Mobley . . .

CURRENT POSITION:

Assistant Attorney General, State of Connecticut, Office of the Attorney General, Department of Children and Families (Hartford, Connecticut)

CAREER HIGHLIGHTS:

Kathryn Mobley has been encouraged by several judges to enter her name for consideration as a member of the bench. Few would guess now that this successful lawyer who has so many challenging options before her once dropped out of law school. But that's how discouraged Kathryn was with a first year of law school marked by rigid teaching methods and a lack of accommodation to her blindness. Kathryn not only returned to law school, however, but went on to positions with Legal Services, with the Social Security Administration, and as a solo practitioner prior to assuming her current role as Assistant Attorney General for the State of Connecticut in 1983.

Although she was born in Los Angeles, California, Kathryn Mobley spent most of her childhood in the rural west. Her early education began in a one-room school house. When she was nine years old, she developed a progressive retinal disease which caused her to lose her sight. At age 14, she moved with her family to Oregon, where she became involved in many high school activities despite her disability.

Kathryn went on to attend Southern Oregon State College, a small liberal arts school. The campus, known for its excellent faculty, provided an environment conducive to learning. In this nurturing atmosphere, Kathryn had the opportunity to hone her leadership skills and to excel academically. "I never saw myself as a leader," she comments, "but I did some things in my senior year that I never thought I could do."

Kathryn found, for example, that she had "the ability to organize people." Following a major environmental symposium on campus, she used this natural talent to get "people with different ideas to agree to an action plan" to implement themes raised in the symposium. In addition, she was also very active as vice president of her class, and she chaired campus campaign efforts on behalf of Bobby Kennedy.

Academically, Kathryn was drawn initially to physics and math. She enjoyed the challenge these subjects posed, but she was discouraged from pursuing a career in science by a teacher who expressed concerns about the safety of a nonsighted person working in a laboratory.

Because she was also "in love with words, the concept of justice, and making a difference," she began to think seriously about a career in the law. Graduating 51/595 in her class with a degree in political science, she obtained a full tuition scholarship to law school.

In 1970, she entered the University of Denver College of Law. The school was very progressive for its time, having admitted five blind students. Only about 5 to 10% of the members of Kathryn's law school class were women—progressive for that time but very different from today's more evenly mixed law school classes. Located in the midst of a large city, the University of Denver offered a sharp contrast to the small college atmosphere of Southern Oregon State. There was no campus and no student union, and the city seemed huge and impersonal with its unfamiliar streets. Living by herself, knowing no one, and feeling very alone, Kathryn attended large first year classes on a tri-semester basis. Some professors' teaching methods were rigid and offered no accommodations for Kathryn's disability. She was expected to quote the law verbatim and recite it in class. Learning the law in this abstract manner seemed meaningless to Kathryn. The "me first" competitive and hostile attitudes of her classmates made the law school environment seem a very different world from the one Kathryn had just left.

To make matters worse, she failed her spring examination in international law. Kathryn had never before failed a test. "The questions seemed like they were from outer space," she recalls. By this point, Kathryn felt law school had managed to "destroy any sense of competence" that she had. The final straw to a bad year came when she fell down a flight of stairs and broke her left ankle. She left campus, never told anyone she was leaving, and literally disappeared. No one ever called to find out why.

For a while, Kathryn did not know what she wanted to do, but in June 1973 she attended a Lion's Club camp for the blind where the only two sighted people were the cook and the nurse. Kathryn returned from camp, she says, "wanting to do something"—and ready to "take on the world again." So she paid a visit to her friends at the Oregon Rehabilitation Center for the Blind. There, she received the help she needed from a very special person in her life—Mr. Kinney. From high school through college, he had been her rehabilitation counselor, and he had always made sure she got the assistance and encouragement she needed. Because of his gruff exterior, Kathryn recalls that Mr. Kinney was not a man you got personally close to, yet she knew he cared and would support her if her plans made sense. By this time, he had become the Executive Director and was no longer able to counsel Kathryn directly. However, Mr. Kinney had learned about her recent difficulties, and this man whom so many considered gruff and intimidating continued to be a major support for Kathryn. Once when she visited the Council a staff member commented, "We were told [by Mr. Kinney] that you were coming and to give you whatever you need the first time you call."

Arrangements were made for Kathryn to finish her law degree. She had to reapply and was accepted. This time things were different. When she first returned to Denver, she stayed with a family, bonded with them for a month, and continued to have Sunday dinner at their home throughout law school. Instead of living alone, she moved into an adult blind home where she had friends and someone to help should she need it. She joined a church in the community and sang in the choir.

Kathryn took the course load of a day student but scheduled as many classes as she could in the evening with adjunct faculty who injected a good dose of "reality" into the study of the law. Being a practical person, she enjoyed these classes much more because the professors de-emphasized theory and focused instead on how the law works, illustrating their points with numerous true life stories about how things work in court. She took civil procedure from a top defense trial lawyer and learned how to advocate for clients. Suddenly, everything seemed completely understandable. Her confidence returned, her grades came up, and she even found time to intern as a law clerk in the local Legal Aid office in order to gain legal experience.

After graduation from law school in 1975, Kathryn worked as a VISTA Volunteer for Legal Aid. In 1976, she moved to the East Coast and took a position as a staff attorney for the Social Security Administration. After leaving the Social Security Administration in 1979, Kathryn worked for three years as a solo practitioner. She then assumed a one-year position as Coordinator for the Connecticut Network Arts for the Handicapped. Following that year, in 1983, Kathryn began work for the Connecticut Attorney General's Office. She has represented many departments and state agencies on environmental issues.

Recently the focus of Kathryn's work has shifted from environmental law to issues involving children. Presently, she is a trial lawyer and handles many parental rights terminations. When a child cannot be cared for properly by his or her parents, Kathryn's role is to litigate to protect the child and free him or her from abuse and neglect. Kathryn finds her present position much different from her previous experience as an environmental lawyer with the state. As an environmental lawyer, her focus was on counseling, on advising, and on reviewing environmental documents for compliance. Now she especially enjoys the pretrial preparation and her actual trial work. Although her current job is extremely demanding, she finds it emotionally rewarding. It "feels good," she says, to be an advocate for children.

Active in the Connecticut and Hartford County Bar Associations, Kathryn finds time to participate in many bar association programs as a panelist, guest speaker, lecturer, and committee chair. Additionally, she has served as a Deacon in her church and as Chair for the Hartford Advisory Commission on the Handicapped.

To help her practice law in a sighted world, Kathryn's constant companion at home, at work, and in court is her Fidelco guide dog, Eli, a German Shepherd, whose daily mission is to make sure Kathryn gets where she needs to go safely. Kathryn also has an assistant who works with her every day—not only at the office but also in court. The assistant's job is to provide support so Kathryn can perform in front of the judge and opposing counsel. This includes keeping documents and exhibits in order and reading last-minute documents to Kathryn when necessary. Kathryn's assistant also takes care of many seemingly simple tasks, from pouring water for Kathryn if she needs a drink of water when she is on trial, to getting lunch while court is in recess, and finding a place to walk Eli. Adept at Braille, Kathryn uses a Braille-and-speak computer which enables her to take notes and draft documents with ease.

To Kathryn, being a successful lawyer is being a good problem solver. She views the law very much as a practical tool for finding solutions. In reviewing cases, Kathryn emphasizes what can be done in the future rather than dwelling on the facts that caused the problem in the first place. Her work is action-oriented, designed to improve the life of her clients.

OTHER TITLES AVAILABLE

The following titles are available at bookstores everywhere:

Guerrilla Tactics For Getting The Legal Job Of Your Dreams —
Regardless of Your Grades, Your School, or Your Work Experience!

National Best Seller. Features hard hitting advice you can put to work immediately.

Author: Kimm Alayne Walton
ISBN: 0-15-900317-2
Price: $24.95
Pages: 556 Pages, 6"x 9"

National Directory Of Legal Employers

Features 22,000 great job openings for law students and recent graduates, including more than 10,000 summer associate positions!

Includes Law Firms, Corporations, Public Interest Organizations and Government Agencies.

Author: The National Association for Law Placement
ISBN: 0-15-900248-6
Price: $39.95
Pages: 1,488 Pages, 8-1/2"x11"

Proceed With Caution —
A Diary Of The First Year At One Of America's Largest, Most Prestigious Law Firms

Author: William F. Keates
ISBN: 0-15-900181-1
Price: $17.95
Pages: 162 Pages, 6" x 9"

America's Greatest Places To Work With A Law Degree —
And How To Make The Most Of Your First Job, No Matter Where It Is!

Author: Kimm Alayne Walton
ISBN: 0-15-900180-3
Price: $24.95
Pages: Approx. 500 Pages, 6"x 9"

For more information or to place an order call 1-800-787-8717, or write: Harcourt Brace Legal & Professional Publications, Inc., 176 West Adams, Suite 2100, Chicago, IL 60603.

Visit our web site at http://www.gilbertlaw.com